ERRATA
Due to an error in the printing process, please note:
p. 16 The first 3 lines are a repetition.
p. 17 The first line should read: "Think about it for a moment:
Children start their records early in life, for example, by telling
the truth or brushing their teeth when they say they will. AT
first you..."
p. 20 The first 2 lines are a repetition.

Getting it Right with Teens

Madelyn Swift

Also by Madelyn Swift

Discipline for Life: Getting it Right with Children

Getting it Right with Teens

Madelyn Swift

Childright
Southlake, Texas

An Essentials Series Book

Childright
2140 East Southlake Boulevard, PMB 640
Southlake, Texas 76092

Printed in the United States of America
First Printing: February, 2000

Library of Congress Cataloging-in-Publication Data
99 096076

Swift, Madelyn
Getting it Right with Teens

ISBN: 1-887069-04-6

The paper used in this publication meets the minimum
requirements of American National Standard for Information
Sciences - Permanence of Paper for Printed Library Materials,
ANZI Z39.48-1984

Childright

This book is dedicated to:
every parent who lives with teens,
Kris & Tim, my favorite teens, and
my husband John, who shared with me
our children's teen years.

Acknowledgments

My first appreciation goes to Vicky Mathies who managed to make my words say what I had originally intended but somehow missed, whose knowledge of this subject is vast, and whose humor and skill dramatically improved this book. Her friendship is invaluable.

Next I wish to thank Julie O'Keefe who organizes my professional life and takes care of me so well that I have time to write. Without her help, this book would never have happened, without her friendship, I would be diminished. To Tammy Stripling and Shelli Thomason, who also pick up so many details for me, I send much appreciation.

Thanks go to the readers who told me what they thought and improved the book: Julie O'Keefe, Brenda Leary, Lynn Deal, Scottie Johnson, Seth Johnson, Marcia Ward, Tina Rivera, Jean Illsley Clarke and Joan Comeau. Thanks to each of you for your wisdom, insights and generosity of spirit.

Special appreciation goes to the teens, friends and family, who talked so openly and honestly and taught me much of what I know about teens: Kris Swift, Tim Swift, Sheila Mathies, Rachel Mathies, Sarah Anderson, Heather McAndrews, Lisa Phillips, Jon Phillips, Mason Gray, Katie Garrity, Jay Stacy and Michael Quentin. Thanks also to Courtney Deal, Mary Wyatt High, Garrett Voorhees and Lauren Brinkmeyer for sharing thoughts. Let anyone question me on whether there are any good teens left: there are and these are some of them!

Finally, I wish to thank my family. I owe a great deal to my sons, Kris and Tim, for reminding me and showing me what teens really are like and for sharing their lives and friends with me. My greatest appreciation goes to my husband John, who makes writing possible, my life happy, and finishing this book a necessity.

Acknowledgments

My first appreciation goes to Vicky Mathies who managed to make my words say what I had originally intended but somehow missed, whose knowledge of this subject is vast, and whose humor and skill dramatically improved this book. Her friendship is invaluable.

Next I wish to thank Julie O'Keefe who organizes my professional life and takes care of me so well that I have time to write. Without her help, this book would never have happened, without her friendship, I would be diminished. To Tammy Stripling and Shelli Thomason, who also pick up so many details for me, I send much appreciation.

Thanks go to the readers who told me what they thought and improved the book: Julie O'Keefe, Brenda Leary, Lynn Deal, Scottie Johnson, Seth Johnson, Marcia Ward, Tina Rivera, Jean Illsley Clarke and Joan Comeau. Thanks to each of you for your wisdom, insights and generosity of spirit.

Special appreciation goes to the teens, friends and family, who talked so openly and honestly and taught me much of what I know about teens: Kris Swift, Tim Swift, Sheila Mathies, Rachel Mathies, Sarah Anderson, Heather McAndrews, Lisa Phillips, Jon Phillips, Mason Gray, Katie Garrity, Jay Stacy and Michael Quentin. Thanks also to Courtney Deal, Mary Wyatt High, Garrett Voorhees and Lauren Brinkmeyer for sharing thoughts. Let anyone question me on whether there are any good teens left: there are and these are some of them!

Finally, I wish to thank my family. I owe a great deal to my sons, Kris and Tim, for reminding me and showing me what teens really are like and for sharing their lives and friends with me. My greatest appreciation goes to my husband John, who makes writing possible, my life happy, and finishing this book a necessity.

Table of Contents

Introduction: Happy Days?
The Teen Years

O nce upon a time we were all teenagers. Mercifully, we have forgotten much of the pain, confusion, and turmoil, as well as the exuberance and vitality, that went along with it. Our memory lapses are most unhelpful to our children who need our compassion, guidance and support as they struggle to find a place for themselves, both within the family and the larger social context.

Don't worry. The teenagers living in your home will force you to examine your past. When they do, don't be selective. Make a conscious effort to recall what it felt like to be 15 or 16 or 17. Were there any hallways in your high school that frightened you? Was there ever an important day in your life when you woke up and found a monstrous crater on your nose that rendered you helpless and distraught? Were there days when it seemed you couldn't control your arms and legs and that everyone noticed and laughed when you tripped on the stairs? Did you check the mirror daily, waiting impatiently for something resembling breasts to grow? Remember the guys at the back of the room who were waiting to pounce on your most minute weakness, expose it to the world, and reduce you to nothingness? Did your "crush" ever sit on the other side of the classroom in Algebra, oblivious to your undying love, and be the cause of your mathematical illiteracy to this day? Did you ever feel like you hadn't a friend in the world, and that nobody understood what you were going through? Think back. It mattered what you wore; it mattered who your friends were; it mattered what you looked like; it mattered how cool you were. It mattered how well you could dribble a basketball, hit a baseball, or how fast you could run. Your world was immediately critical, but not immediately forgiving.

Now, remember your parents.
Hey, that's you now.

Nobody wants to see a child suffer and struggle. None of us wishes to believe that our children are going to fall prey to the whims of peer pressure and the flightiness of the social mores of the day. We want to believe that our children are going to meet some 1950's television family image of the well-adjusted, happy, productive, self-sufficient and polite teenager. Some of the time they will be all of these things, but other times they won't even come close. Our children, like us, are human; they come complete with all the frailties and imperfections with which we ourselves struggle. We are not perfect, and neither are they. One of the most loving gifts we can give our teenagers is our understanding of what it feels like to be bombarded by conflicting information

from all sides, what it is like to struggle against difficult, available and compelling temptations, what it is like to experience the betrayals of friendship, and both the joys and pain of first love. To begin to appreciate their experience, and then to offer the appropriate kinds of support, guidance and structure, we need to know some of what is going on developmentally between the ages of roughly thirteen to nineteen. Many of the changes in these years are obvious, others not so.

We, and they, can see that they are changing. Hormones rule their world. To say teens are hormonally challenged is an understatement. They achieve their adult height and acquire external sexual characteristics; the bone structures of their faces take on the shapes they will live with for the rest of their lives. Unfortunately, the rates of growth vary widely in this age group. Some will look like adults by fourteen, while others will have only the rudimentary beginnings of pubertal development. Indeed, within even one teen's growth there can be uncomfortable inconsistencies. A boy may grow tall, but acquire slowly the pubic and facial hair, muscular development, and penile growth which is so important to his image of himself as masculine. If they grow too rapidly, they may not be able to gain control over their new large and unfamiliar limbs. Similarly, when boys are slow in gaining their adult height, they may feel inferior, less capable, and less desirable than their taller peers. They may become the object of merciless teasing and belittling which can make life feel unliveable. Teens can seem to be without mercy or empathy at this stage. They are all uncomfortable.

Girls with early breast development may feel self-conscious and embarrassed; those with no breasts crave nothing more than to fill out a bra. And, no matter what we as adults think about it, girls want to look like the magazine image of a beautiful woman. They wish to have the look and size which are seen by their social group to be desirable. They are painfully aware that you cannot change your bone structure and the face that your parents lovingly gave you, and yet, that is what they desire above all else. Similarly, they wish to be sexual beings, but struggle with understanding the realities (timing, birth control, sexually transmitted diseases) and acquiring the maturity that a sexual relationship demands. This is true for both boys and girls. The gap between who they are and who they wish to be is huge and can be damaging to already precarious self-image and self-esteem.

Please also keep in mind that these times are not all bad. The teenage years are filled with more energy and creativity than are rarely available again. Excitement, joy and true connection with others abound. Understanding and perspective expand geometrically. So much meaning, so much purpose, so much potential; the world is yet theirs to discover and grasp. They have yet to choose what mark they shall make in the world, and they dream of making differences that count. Their unfolding is rapid-paced; so are their lives. And I am pretty certain that teens have lots more fun than grownups: they often seem to laugh more and to taste life more fully. Charles Dickens, referring to French Revolutionary times in *A Tale of Two Cities*, perhaps best described adolescence:

> It was the best of times, it was the worst of times, it was the age of wisdom, it was the age of foolishness, it was the epoch of belief, it was the epoch of incredulity, it was the season of Light, it was the season of Darkness, it was the spring of hope, it was the winter of despair, we had everything before us, we had nothing before us, we were all going direct to Heaven, we were all going direct the other way—in short, the period was so far like the present period, that some of its noisiest authorities insisted on its being received, for good or for evil, in the superlative degree of comparison only.

To us grownups it would seem that teens live in the superlative. This must be somewhere we have not been for awhile, because we seem to have trouble connecting with them some days. We also have a fair amount of trouble keeping up with them.

Not surprisingly, although it may often seem not to be so to us as parents, our teenagers are entering a period of rapid intellectual growth. As psychologist Peter Marshall[1] reports:

> One of the most important and dramatic changes that takes place in adolescents is that

they become capable of sophisticated and rational thinking. While I am the first to acknowledge that, at times, it may seem that teenagers have left, rather than entered, an age of reason, I assure you this is not the case. I would also like to convince you that much of the insecurity and conflict that can be experienced by teenagers is, in fact, the result of their ability to think in different and more complex ways."

Teenagers are often argumentative and critical—of our ideas, our beliefs, even our appearance. This is particularly uncomfortable for us as parents, but we need to understand that this is a period when young people challenge any and all beliefs, even their own, in an attempt to arrive at some final personal definitions and understanding of their world. Needless to say, one of the things that we will discuss later in this book is helping them to express their disagreement and pursuit of freedom and self-identity in ways which are neither dangerous to themselves, nor destructive of their families and the society in which they must become active and contributing participants.

For most teens, however, their peer group is of the utmost importance. Most spend their every waking moment trying to be cool. It is obvious that young teens have no idea how to manage this, while older teens, once they start to "get it right," begin to determine what is cool for those who follow. It is at this stage when so many parents turn dumb— well, at least according to their teenage children. (You will get smarter again sometime in your child's twenties.) Their peers know more. During one shopping trip, my adolescent sons told me that I did not know what cool was. I could only reply that I did once, a long time ago. (If you are going to live with teens, you had better have a sense of humor, especially about yourself.) I neglected to mention that I no longer cared. This most certainly would be true sacrilege to a teen.

A teen's goal is to attain her freedom and to make her own decisions. This is also the hallmark of our struggle with them. Determining which freedoms should come at what times is difficult for every family. It is a critical and recurring problem which we must face. How we handle handing over these increasing freedoms will foretell and direct much of our relationship with them. Since seeking freedom is one of the primary developmental tasks of this age group, one of the biggest mistakes many of us make is to continue to try to control or direct a teen's life as we did when they were small and vulnerable. For others, the mistake will be to abdicate our role as parents and abandon our teens to their own devices, to believe they will "catch on" by themselves, to give them too much freedom too rapidly. Our letting go, and their acquisition, of freedom must be a step-by-step process; they do not just figure everything out right away and take over beautifully when they are eighteen or twenty-one. They have to practice handling varying responsibilities and aspects of their lives in ever increasing increments. This means that the parent of a teen must let go of what she previously controlled and directed in her child's younger life. For some parents this is excruciatingly difficult and painfully frightening. But it must happen.

Despite the fact that we adults often view a teenager's separation and identity-seeking behavior as rebellion, it is more often an attempt to find her own unique identity. We must be careful in our perceptions and judgments. In order to become a full-fledged adult, one has to separate, and be different in some ways, from parents. It is what we all did in becoming our own person. When we learn to adapt to this changing relationship, watching our child grow can be one of the most exciting and rewarding times of our lives.

Sophisticated and worldly in many ways, teenagers can be extremely naive in others.

> They are a mix of child and grownup. Trying to determine which persona will surface next is virtually impossible. They wish to be treated like adults but act like children. Who wouldn't?

They hate it when we are right and they hate when we are wrong. Confusion is certainly an integral part of adolescence. Let us take a look at what we can do to reduce our own confusion and guide our teens through these tumultuous years.

Please keep in mind that this book, indeed no book, can *make* great teens. Our working towards creating independent and responsible adults begins when they are born. The better we, as parents, set the stage prior to the teen years, the greater the probability that the teen years will be less bumpy. Discipline, communication, in short all of our interactions with our children, are investments towards their teen and adult years. This book's purpose is to help parents become better parents of teens, to feel more confident as parents of teens, and to make living with teens more comfortable and easier. It is my hope that this book can help to make the transition from parent-child relationship to the parent-teen relationship go more smoothly. We parents are responsible for selecting the process; our teens must be in charge of the outcome.[2] I wish, like most parents, that I could make my children's lives run perfectly and according to some perfect vision. But we cannot. Just as we cannot protect our children from unhappiness and discomfort, we cannot *make* these teen years free from the odd bump and rough climb upwards. Our goal is to determine what *our* response will be to these bumps: the rest is up to them.

Chapter 1:
Freedom and Responsibility

Teen Comments

"What my parents did right was that they gave me the room to fall on my face, or at least enough to let me think that I was, but were close enough to catch me when I needed it. They were like the spotters for a gymnast on a balance beam. And, of course, they're still doing this, and probably always will. It's nice to know that I have the freedom to try new things and do things my own way, but if I mess up, I also have a support system."
—Sheila, 18

Teaching teens the connection between their freedom and their level of demonstrated responsibility is essential, not only to their development, but to discipline. Every teenager with whom I spoke placed freedom at the top of his list of not simply desirables, but essentials for growing up and for living together. Freedom is what all children, indeed all human beings, not just teens seek. Understanding the issues around freedom is a huge key to understanding teens. For them, appreciating the link between freedom and responsibility is one of the steps to understanding how to obtain freedom. Give them this key, and teach them how to use it.

First, let us look at how the whole freedom and responsibility link provides a working framework for self-discipline. The good news is that all teens will give us an opportunity to share this lesson or key with them. The following story was my clarifying event; it is told also in *Discipline for Life: Getting it Right with Children* because of its universal quality. When our youngest son Tim was twelve, he looked at me one day and in total frustration said, "I just want you off my case and out of my life." Sound familiar? Somehow, I found the truth and grace (rare for me) I needed. I looked him straight in the eyes and replied, "Tim, you don't seem to understand; we both want the same thing." (First, I could be doing something else besides disciplining him, and second, the goal here is self-discipline which by definition includes me out of his life, in the way Tim means it, and off his case.) "I want this so much I'm going to tell you how to get it. All you have to do is handle your life responsibly and I back out of it a step. Handle it again responsibly and I back out farther. You could choose to handle your life responsibly from this moment on and have me out of it—complete freedom if you will. However (and the 'however' was necessary because at twelve, we all know he could not pull this off), should you handle your life irresponsibly, you will have sent me an engraved invitation back into your life. And because I'm your mother, I will accept it, and I will be there." This is my job, and I take it very seriously.

The principle we have been examining is best stated as: the greater the level of proven responsibility, the greater the level of extended freedom. As one's taking of responsibility expands, so too does the freedom which can be given. Of course, should the teen's carrying of responsibility be lacking, so too will the freedom they are afforded. Bringing up children (from our perspective) and attaining freedom and autonomy (from their perspective) can be as simple as this.

Freedom is defined by Webster's Collegiate Dictionary[3] as *the absence of coercion or constraint in choice or action.* In other words, freedom is the power to choose what one does or says. From the toddler who would eat nothing but cookies, to the child who would never come in from outside, to the teen who wants to go with his friends whenever and wherever he chooses, kids seek freedom and view grownups as an interference in their lives and a barrier to happiness—at the very least, to their self-satisfaction. We prevent them from making their own decisions: we offer only healthy foods at mealtime, we don't allow them to ride their bicycles on busy roads, and we keep them in until they finish homework. We are no fun at all. Of course, we are only doing our job as parents.

By no means is it being suggested that we should let children make these decisions. What is true is that most of them *want* to make these decisions and, furthermore, think they are quite capable of doing so. This is where the controversy and confusion begin. Frequently, a child views himself as capable of making a specific decision, while the parent does not.

Sometimes, we know for certain that they are not ready. Young children should not choose when to go to bed, how much junk food they may eat, when to brush their teeth; teens are legally not allowed to choose when they are ready to drive, nor should they be entirely in charge of household rules, curfews and family values. Like it or not (for both them and us), it is a parent's job to say no in these situations and to deny freedom. Period. No must mean no!

As children age, however, more and more of life's decisions become theirs to make. The determination of when to allow them a particular freedom or decision-making power can be difficult. If, however, they do not practice and thus learn to make choices and to handle increasing freedoms at home, when and where will they learn to handle their lives? If they did not practice decision-making early in their lives, encouraging and allowing them to begin to make decisions as teens is important; the learning steps must be taken. It is in everyone's best interest, but especially the teen's, to make some important life decisions. These will range from deciding what his room and hair look like, to when and how much homework to do, to what music he likes, to whether to have sex with his girlfriend. (You weren't thinking he would ask your permission on this one were you?) Hopefully, you will have had numerous discussions, not lectures, about sex. You will have shared your values, his values and his friends' values and viewpoints on abstinence, birth control, the real dangers of sexually transmitted diseases, and the life-altering effects of getting pregnant and having a child. This way your voice will have been heard before the decision-making takes place and the decision is made.

Before we get to these important decisions, we need our children to have practiced, and succeeded and failed, at handling increasingly more important life decisions while they were young so that they are wiser, more experienced decision-makers as they enter into life-altering and life-threatening decisions. They will have to decide whether to continue their education, and if so, how much of their time will be devoted to studying and partying at college, as well as how they will handle drugs, drinking and driving, and their sex lives. As frightening as it may be, these decisions are *theirs* to make. It is our job as parents to ensure that our sons and daughters are excellent problem-solvers and decision-makers *before* they reach these types of decisions. If you have not already begun doing this, start now. It is also our job then to let go of the decision-making. Some of us decision-makers *before* they reach these types of decisions. If you have not already begun doing this, start now. It is also our job then to let go of the decision-making. Some of us will find letting go extremely difficult. Some of us will abdicate it much too soon.

Determine When and What to Let Go

What can help us let go? When the issue is not clear or when there exists controversy over what is best, appropriate or allowable, we need a method for clarifying, predicting and making a decision. There are three steps to clarifying: 1)the teen's proven track record, 2)the teen's ability to describe how this new level of freedom will be handled responsibly, and 3)an evaluation of this trial.

First of all, a teen needs to have proven with actions that she is, and has been responsible, to the current level of freedom she holds. For example, she must have driven safely with a parent in the car for several months before driving alone can even be considered. Or your son must have handled himself at a friend's house in town before staying with friends out of town. (It is much easier to "go fetch" in town than out.) She must have watched movies with vulgar language and not altered her language or her behavior to be allowed to go to PG-13 and more restricted movies. Maintaining a proven track record, if possible in the same or similar area of responsibility, is step one. This record must already be in place and comfortably established.

need to check those teeth. Soon, you only need to check periodically, and later, results at the dentist's office tell the whole story. If no cavities have occurred, then the child can maintain the right and freedom to brush his teeth on his own without your reminding or checking. Similarly, when a child consistently stops at the edge of the sidewalk before crossing the street with you, you can begin to watch him cross by himself. Later this same child will have earned the freedom to go to his friend's house all by himself. Again, a step by step proven track record has been developing. If this same child fails to stop at the edge while you are watching, he goes back to waiting to cross with you. Going to his friend's house alone will have to wait. Once again, if the child demonstrates a lack of responsibility, he loses his freedom. We need to send this message: act irresponsibly, and you invite me back into your life. It is always the child's choice.

Second, to prove capability, a teen needs to describe how he will handle a new freedom responsibly. A technique called "convince me"[4] can be quite useful here. Your sixteen-year-old daughter wants to go into the center of the city for a major concert. You are worried about safety and tempted to say no but realize you have no real justification for doing so except you would prefer her not to go. What are you to do?

It is important for us to teach our children that we have three answers to their requests: yes, no, and convince me. "Yes" makes everyone happy and causes no problems. "No" is the one our children hate. We not only have a right to say no, we are obliged to say it to keep our children out of physically, emotionally or socially dangerous situations. As well, it is essential that our children are denied inappropriate requests (junk food before dinner, watching television rather than doing homework) and learn to accept the reality that life does not always go their way. This is an extremely valuable lesson to learn in life; the earlier one comes to grips with this concept, the earlier one begins to develop another helpful life skill, handling frustrating and disappointing situations with some grace.

When you are uncertain as to what your response to the request should be, especially uncertain as to whether your child can handle this new freedom, and wish to avoid saying no arbitrarily, try saying the third answer, "convince me." Remember the burden of proof rests with your child; it is your teen's job to do the convincing. Please note this is quite different from saying no first and then being negotiated, cajoled or bargained out of your position. Teach your child how to respond. Responses that will not work include all of the responses from their viewpoint, such as, "Everyone else's Mom is letting them go" (like I care), "I really love this band" (buy the CD), and "I'll be your best friend" (oh, please). The answers that are more likely to convince us come from our perspective. We parents are concerned about danger and safety. Answers that have a probability of working include, "We will take Christina's new Suburban. All six of us will stay together all of the time. Two of the guys are over six feet tall. We will take two mobile phones and call when we are on our way back. We will be home by 1:00 a.m." It is hard to argue when our teens have anticipated the dangers and taken responsibility for their own safety. Please remember, if your child's responses do not allow you to feel comfortable giving permission, don't give it. Say no.

There is a bonus to your child learning this lesson. It includes the skill of learning to view situations through others' eyes, and meeting their needs as the situation demands. For example, when a prospective employer interviews your son and asks why she should give him this job, your son does not answer, "Because I really really want it." Instead, he will say, "I will be here every day on time; I am dependable. I will do what is necessary to complete all tasks; I am a hard worker. Also, I am a quick study and will be easy to train."

Don't forget to take the time to evaluate this increased freedom. If your teen is successful and handles herself responsibly (dependably and honestly), this success and freedom are added to her track record. If, on the other hand, she fails to call, takes an unsafe car, or uses drugs at the concert (an act both irresponsible and illegal), she will lose ground in her freedoms. She may be limited to home or the concert (an act both irresponsible and illegal), she will lose ground in her freedoms. She may be limited to home or to school events until she again successfully improves her track record, and we, the parents, are again comfortable allowing this freedom. Let your children know that their handling a new freedom poorly makes us all a little skittish; we are less likely to extend freedom again soon.

> We have not passed that subtle line between childhood and adulthood until we move from the passive voice to the active voice—that is, until we have stopped saying "It was lost," and say, "I lost it." —Sydney J. Harris, *On the Contrary*

Keys to Freedom
⚷   Teach: "Handle your life responsibly, gain more freedom. Handle it irresponsibly, lose some." Teach your children exactly how to get you out of their lives. What a gift for both of you!
⚷   Teach your teens to make you, their parents, so comfortable with their capabilities and "convince me" proofs that you can't say no.

Chapter Checkpoints

✔   All children, including teens, seek freedom. From a child's perspective, grownups seek to invade their space and to inhibit their freedom.

✔   Teach the link between freedom and responsibility: responsible decisions and actions are the steps on the path to freedom.

✔   Children and teens often perceive themselves as ready for a particular freedom before the grownup does. The burden of proof rests with the teen. This is an opportunity, not a restriction or punishment.

✔   When unsure whether a teen is ready for a specific freedom, 1)check the proven track record, 2)use "convince me," and 3)evaluate the progress.

✔   Teen track records of responsibility and irresponsibility have been built daily from the time they were very young. Help them understand how they can make you so comfortable, you can only say yes.

Chapter 2:
Freedom and Trust

Teen Comments

"I have one friend whose parents seriously don't think that she has ever had anything to drink. The other week she tasted wine "for the first time." I would hate having to lie to my parents that much. I do think that there should be rules, but I don't think that they should interfere totally with a child's social life, and I don't think that they should drive a teen to do what they want anyway, but behind your back and without your knowing about it. These parents often don't really know where she is because she knows that if she told them she wouldn't be allowed out.... She wouldn't be allowed to go somewhere if there were going to be boys there and no parents. This rules out almost every party I've ever been to. You see what I'm driving at."
—*Sheila, 18*

"The best thing that parents do is trust their kids. My parents did and I 'think' that I turned out alright!"
—*Natalie, 20*

"Don't make your kids lie to you by not letting them do anything because if they are forced to do so, they will. Remember kids are the most resourceful and knowledgeable people alive when it comes to keeping their freedom and knowing just how their parents operate." —Tim, 18

Freedom and trust are as tightly interwoven as freedom and responsibility. The trust which is based on a solid experience of honesty is the second key to obtaining freedom. This key must also be taught to teens and like the first key, responsibility, trust can be taught even when they are young. It, too, is associated with a track record that is built over time. Unhappily, trust is broken quickly, but built slowly.

Trust is an essential element of all healthy relationships. Simply put, a healthy relationship cannot exist without trust. The fundamental lesson our children must learn concerning dishonesty is that lying breaks trust. Relationships depend on trust. Lying shatters the foundation of a relationship. As my child, you are one person with whom I must have a relationship, a healthy relationship; you are entirely too important to me to have that damaged in any way. Therefore, my only option is to teach you how to rebuild my trust and, thus, form and maintain a healthy relationship between us.

Lying destroys trust quickly and efficiently. It takes but one deception to undermine trust. Trust must be whole and complete; there is no, "I sort of trust you." Either I can trust you or I can't.

There are a variety of clever ways to lie. One can lie blatantly with audacity, "I didn't do it" or "I will never do it again"; with tricky language, "I didn't mean to" or "I thought you said I could" or "You didn't say I couldn't" or "Samantha said it would be okay"; or by omission, "We went to Ann's and played soccer and talked." Unspoken here is the fact that "we" also went to a restricted movie which this teen had been forbidden to see. Anytime someone has allowed, encouraged or led another to believe something is true which is not, lying is involved. There are no little lies; when the trust between us is broken, it is no small offense. It may seem strange, but we must describe and explain to our children all of these methods of deception so that we have been clear what lying includes. Let there be no misunderstanding.

Freedom is dependent upon trust. If I cannot believe you when you tell me where you will be, what you will do, with whom you will be, how can I in good conscience let you go? Teach this to your child. It is our job as parents to know what they are doing and who they really are out there in the world.

Once a child breaks our trust with a deception, his job becomes the rebuilding of trust. He does this by telling the truth repeatedly and without exception and by doing what he says he will do. This takes time and assessment.

Don't expect your trust to return easily or quickly. Of course, the younger the child, the more quickly we need to let trust be rebuilt. Most children try lying. After all, not owning the truth can be a way out of trouble, a way to avoid harsh punishment, a way not to own something we wish we hadn't done, a way to look better, or a way to get what we want. We have all been tempted to lie; most of us have given in to it, but the older we are, the larger the digression becomes. We should, and do, know better. Even young children can be and need to be taught that there is no misdeed or offense as big as the lie surrounding it.

> The lie is always worse than what you have done.

As a child earns and rebuilds trust step by step, incident by incident, the parent can begin to return freedom to him incrementally.

For example, a teen lies about where he will go or has gone with his friends for an evening. This is when "grounding" is appropriate. Since the teen cannot be trusted, he needs to stay close to home and go only to school and work, if he has a job. After a time, perhaps a week or two, we can begin to look at school-related events or doing homework with a friend which can be checked up on, and check up we need to do.

A teen who has lied and violated trust needs to understand that she has invited you back into her life. Having an eye kept on her and being checked randomly to determine that she is where she said she would be are essential to returning to a firm basis of trust. Will a teen resent this? Yes, but keeping tabs is our job and necessary. When checking by telephone, please remember to call and ask to speak to your son or daughter. Do not tell anyone that you are just checking up on your child. The goal is never to embarrass our child; in fact, the goal needs to be to cause as little humiliation as possible. We are just trying to teach a lesson here. The first part of the lesson is that violating trust with dishonesty seriously hurts our relationship. The second part of the lesson is that trust takes time and a number of consecutive truths to be rebuilt. For a parent to know for certain that his teen is telling the truth, checking up on her is necessary. After this teenaged daughter has rebuilt her record of honesty, checking is no longer necessary until and unless this child gives us a reason (lying, inappropriate behavior, drastic changes in behavior, etc.) to do so again.

Teach your child that breaking our trust and shattering the parent-child relationship is a most destructive situation, and one to be avoided. Telling the truth is always better, no matter what the original violation was. Truth and freedom are inextricably bound together and spiral into either heavenly or hellish times for parents and their teenaged children.

From the teen point of view, parents most often direct the spiral downward either by not believing anything they say and assuming they are always untrustworthy or by not trusting or allowing them to do anything. In this case, they all say it is worth it to lie to have a life. Most teens seem to recognize the positive spiral that honesty and trust form. If parents start out trusting children and their young teens to be honest and responsible, kids tend to want to live up to this. They actually want to be as honest and responsible as often and as much as they can. Informed and aware parental trust leads to teen honesty which leads to more trust which leads to more honesty and responsibility which leads to more trust and freedom which ... and on and on. This is the helpful and easy-to-live-with spiral.

It can, of course, spiral the other way. Not trusting your children leads them to be untrustworthy and dishonest; they will live up to this expectation as well. This only makes you trust them less which leads to more dishonesty which leads to less trust ... and on and on. This is clearly a spiral to avoid. Instead, teach the link between trust and honesty and healthy relationships. This negative spiral is a difficult one to pull out of, difficult but not impossible. The journey back begins with either party taking the first step towards trust or honesty. This is generally very scary for both parties, but it is certainly worth the effort.

> Remember, teens will pay almost any price for their freedom, even telling the truth.
> Make it the price.

We, the parents, are responsible for teaching the lessons involved in the Freedom-Trust connection. The earlier we teach that trust is fundamental to our relationship, that dishonesty destroys trust, and that trust can be rebuilt with effort, the more easily and quickly our children come to understanding better choices and their own role in achieving the much sought after freedom. We must always remember that being honest ourselves, scrupulously honest, is essential to teaching this lesson. We too must earn trustworthiness.

Four essential parent skills contribute directly to a child's developing trustworthiness and honesty as life skills. These are: 1)Be honest, 2)Say YES whenever you can, 3)Respect them, and 4)Listen to them (Chapters 2, 3, 4, and 6 respectively).

Reasons Teens Lie to Parents

❶   Teens lie to get what they want, especially to get to do what they want to do; this is quite often something not yet allowed by their parents.

❷   Teens lie to avoid owning a poor choice or action which either does not fit into their parents' or their own view of themselves, or which diminishes their self-respect or self-esteem. In other words, temptation called to them, and they answered and now sincerely wish they had not.

❸   Teens lie because they believe their parents don't *ever* trust them (dishonesty ⇨ mistrust ⇨ dishonesty spiral)—so there is no point in telling the truth. Some teens have become so used to lying that they lie even when there is no reason or need.

❹   Teens lie to stay out of trouble. They want to keep their freedom. They also, not surprisingly, lie to avoid consequences, discipline or harsh punishment.

❺   Teens lie so that they look better to their peers.

Chapter Checkpoints

✔   Trust is an essential, fundamental element of emotionally healthy relationships.

✔   Dishonesty shatters trust. There are no small white lies.

✔   The teen's job is to build or rebuild trust. This requires time, repeated truthful incidents, and parental assessment.

✔   Recognize and teach the two spirals:
       1) dishonesty ⇨ mistrust ⇨ dishonesty
       2) honesty ⇨ trust ⇨ honesty
Avoid the first; seek and build the second.

✔   The price of freedom is honesty; it is a fair price. Freedom is a valuable commodity, especially to teens. Teach them to get it the old-fashioned way: earn it.

✔   Each of us has been tempted by dishonesty. Our understanding can be a powerful tool.

✔   Honesty isn't the best policy; it is the *only* policy.

Chapter 3:
Say YES Whenever You Can

Teen Comments

"One thing that I noticed in high school about something that parents did wrong were the ones that kept a leash on the kids and were overprotective! You know the kind that questions you if you aren't home like ten minutes after the movie is over on Friday night because that is only how long it should take you to get home. I had a friend in high school whose parents did this. She couldn't even come over to my house unless there were parents there to supervise ... and I am not talking freshman year, this continued into her junior and senior year. They also wouldn't let her be at the movies only with someone of the opposite sex. She had to have friends escort her." —Natalie, 20

"I think my parents are good because they were lenient enough for me to experience a lot of independence, but not enough to get in too much trouble." —Sarah, 20

Firrst let's talk about saying no. You must be able to say no and mean it and follow through to be an effective parent of young children or teens. Say no when there is danger—to others, to things, to themselves, to their emotional health, and also to risks to their character development. *For the love of your children, say no.* Be their parent, not their friend. (This does not preclude your being friendly to each other.) You are not peers. When their request is inappropriate, say no so they learn one of life's most important lessons: life is not always going to go your way. You also give them boundaries within which they may operate. This provides a sense of security and reconfirms your love for them. You do have their best interests at heart.

Alternatively, say yes or convince me whenever you can. Teach your teens that you will say no based almost exclusively on danger or for previous irresponsibility. If you can show me (convince me) how you will make yourself as safe as possible or immune from the danger or how you will handle a situation responsibly, I will say yes to requests, even though my mommy-heart is still somewhat scared to do so. If you consistently do this and your teens know your record, they have less need to lie. They can more easily predict when you will say yes. They also realize deep in their hearts that if you do say no to a request, it is likely a bad, or dangerous, or perhaps morally wrong idea. If we lead our children to emotional health, they are neither self-destructive nor stupid. They are simply seeking freedom.

Teens want and need expanding privileges. As long as they have that proven track record of responsibility and trust, they should receive these. When our children know that if they can minimize the risk (letting them drive to the grocery store to get milk is not without risk anymore) to themselves, we will likely come through for them, they have little need to lie to us. Here are some examples to accomplish this.

Early in their teen years, our sons wanted to see movies of which I did not approve, largely for reasons of language and violence. These I considered to be threats to their character development. As they had demonstrated with television programs, their personal levels of swearing, disrespect, and aggressive actions did not increase after viewing. (I should note that their behavior most certainly had deteriorated after this kind of viewing when they were younger, and they had been prohibited from watching many programs because of this.) However, this was no longer true. Based on their track record of not altering their language or actions even after watching undesirable behavior, I allowed them to see some movies which were not my first choices. I had no reason to say no. Their character values, and behavior were no longer threatened by viewing. Even if I do not enjoy those types of movies, they may.

Later, they wanted to go into the city closest to us, Dallas, to attend concerts. Now every mother knows that if your child goes into the big city, any big city, they are never coming back alive. We just know these things. My first inclination was of course to say, "No, you'll be killed!" However, I did manage "Convince me." They were ready. As reported in the "Freedom and Responsibility" chapter, they convinced me with cell phones, safe cars, staying together and a curfew. They also related a story about that concert which helped form my policy to say yes when I could. Two female friends really wanted to see this band, *really* wanted to see this band. They also knew they would be told no; they were not yet allowed to go into Dallas on their own at night. After all, this is a difficult decision and freedom to give. These girls were clever but imprudent. Each asked her parents if she could spend the night at the other's house. Each received permission. They then proceeded to go into the city and stay at the concert until its end. Then, having nowhere to go, they spent the night in their car in Dallas. This was not wise, and certainly more dangerous than attending the concert. Teens will lie to get to do something they really want to do. This excuses neither the lying nor the overnight in the car; our goal is to prevent both of these from happening.

What can a parent do? Several things. First, teach "convince me" so that kids have a shot at getting what they want and learn how to get it when possible. This technique also teaches other skills: planning, creative problem solving, anticipating possible outcomes, and developing realistic plans for dealing with them. Second, teach them to earn freedom and trust. If you lie, you will be watched like a hawk until you regain trust. This will not be fun. Third, teach them to be creative with problem solving. The girls who wanted to see the concert might have arranged to have an older sibling or friend take them and have received parental approval. And fourth, when you do feel you need to say no (it is a legitimate and allowable answer and quite dependent on the age and maturity of the teen), be aware of what is happening in their lives. You need to know that temptation has called; help them avoid it. Teens do not lose face for having smart parents who recognize temptation and follow through on having said no. "It's not worth it. My dad will check up on me; I'll get caught. I wish I had dumb parents." If the girls had known they might be checked up on at the other's house, this lie would not have been an option. No lost face, just "bad" luck of the draw on parents.

Every teen I interviewed said that their friends whose parents did not allow them to do much of anything lied. Even the "good" kids, the solid, responsible teens, said they didn't blame their peers for this. The consensus was that everyone needed and deserved a life. (Read "increasing freedom" for "a life" here.) Kids who weren't allowed one, obtained one by doing whatever it took. This always seemed to include lying. The solid teens also noted that the parents had received what they deserved and earned. All of the teens were aware that not being allowed some freedom (in a situation where you had not blown it) was demeaning and demoralizing. They also realized that parents cannot protect their children from everything, nor should they. Some day these very children will need to be able to handle themselves in the real world. They will have needed steady incremental practice to do so.

These same older teens (18 and 19) said that in hindsight, they were glad their parents had also known when to say no. Limits are important and helpful. Finding the balance is the key.

Chapter Checkpoints
✔   Say NO in cases of danger to physical well-being, emotional health, or character development.
✔   Say YES whenever possible. Proven track records are very helpful here. So is remembering what it was like to be a teen.
✔   Use "CONVINCE ME" when you are uncertain.

Chapter 4:
Respect Them

Teen Comments

"They gave me a lot of opportunities that allowed me to figure out my own interests and successes." —Lauren, 19

"It is important for mutual respect to exist between a parent and a child. Without it, honesty is a challenge. With mutual respect, I am more inclined to be honest and open with anyone, but especially parents." —Heather, 20

"My mom knows that I won't have the same values and ideas as her. She gives me advice and raises me to come up with my own ideas about life. I know that she respects our similarities as well as our differences." —Mary, 16

Respect is defined[5] as *considering something or someone worthy of high regard or refraining from interfering with someone or one's privacy.* Respect is a key ingredient in any relationship; without respect there is never much of a true relationship. Respecting someone in our hearts and actually consistently showing respect to another are two different things. Some parents struggle with only the second, showing respect. Others grapple with both—feeling, as well as showing, respect. It is guaranteed that if you don't feel respectful toward someone, you aren't showing respect.

Being treated with respect was an issue brought up by several of the teens I interviewed. Each acknowledged that his parents had at times missed on this, but the teens who spoke highly of their parents conceded that their parents, on the whole, had done their utmost to be respectful toward their children. This seemed to count big for the teens. As parents, what do we need to respect about children?

Existence
Well, first of all, we need to value and respect them purely because they are, because they exist. This means considering them worthy of high regard. They are. We have overrated self-worth based on accomplishments for too long. Our teens, indeed all of us, need to understand that we have considerable worth simply because we exist, apart from what we do, whether we succeed or fail. That is not to say that effort and accomplishment are not important. However, it is only by offering our children worth based on existence that they become much more free to risk failure and try for success. With the incredible pressure placed on teens to achieve, it behooves us to stress existence. This is a stance

that a helpful parent must take; this attitude needs to be present. Children of all ages sense it; teens hone right in on it and are keenly aware when it is missing.

As discussed in *Discipline for Life: Getting it Right with Children,*[6] respect is an often overlooked ingredient in cooperation. When any of us cooperates, when there is neither coercion nor manipulation taking place, it is because we choose to do so. And we choose to cooperate because we have been treated respectfully. When anyone violates our dignity, treats us disrespectfully, we feel like working against them not with them. If you expect cooperation from your teen, then you must treat her with respect. We must also somehow manage to show respect even when we are angry; this models anger management and grace under fire—both ever so helpful life skills.

Different from Us

We must also respect their need and right to be themselves and different from us. Too often we witness parents living vicariously through a child or teen; too often parents expect teens to have exactly the same ideas, philosophies and values. A teen's job is to rethink all of these so that he can choose his own and internalize them. Those values which are internally derived, which come from inside us, are far more likely to last and to be lived out than those that were imposed from outside and never personally evaluated and integrated. We spend years helping our children learn to think, and then we grow fearful that they actually will. In actuality, children have a disturbing tendency to grow up like their parents—not like who their parents say they are but who they really are and how they act.

> Living our values is the surest route to having our children accept them as their own.

Not only will our teens' values vary somewhat from our own, their personality characteristics will too. If you are a Type A driven, ambitious parent who has a Type B laid-back, live-in-the-moment child, you may struggle with allowing this teen to be herself. The organized one struggles with disorganized, neat with messy, athletes with non-athletes, readers with non-readers, etc. It is a natural inclination to believe our children will be like us, and when they are young, they sometimes are. Of course, some parents are given such good lessons in I-am-not-you by their young children that they learn early that this child is different.

My friend Vicky's daughter Sheila taught her this lesson when she was only six years old. Vicky had come of age in a time when it seemed a wonderful new right to wear non-stereotypical female clothing, and she loved the freedom this afforded her. Sheila, however, was one of those little girls who lived for frilly tights, swirling dresses, and silky shawls and who thought denim overalls an unnecessary aberration. As Sheila's individual tastes began to express themselves, Vicky had to accept that it was her daughter's right to determine her own brand of femininity and appearance. Sheila had to be allowed, even encouraged, to develop her own particular individual expression. And, true to form, Sheila has not been led by her mother's clothing tastes nor her peers'; she defines her own style today as a young adult.

Still other children let us believe that their values are just like our values, and we allow ourselves to get comfortable. Discovering during the teen years, that your son does not care about baseball anymore can be quite a shock to some parents. We need to let them be themselves. Don't you wish people would stop "helping" you or trying to change you?

Their Ideas

We will also need to respect their ideas. Dismiss a teen's ideas often enough, and he will begin to doubt his mind and his ability to think. When this disapproval and rejection come from a parent, they are even more devastating. We all had strange ideas in high school and college that we managed to think our way through; so, too, will your teen. The teen years are all about trying on ideas, behaviors, traits, and looks. This is how we separate from parents, or put another way, find our true selves; it is a very important developmental task.

Right to Make Decisions and Mistakes

Every teen I talked with mentioned their need to make decisions and their need and right to make short term mistakes in their lives. Each recognized that making mistakes is part of the learning and growing-up process. Each strongly desired the right to fall on his face even knowing how much it would hurt. They also seemed to recognize that when they did manage to get things right, they owned that success. Repeatedly, these teens amazed me with their insights.

Space and Time

Their space and time must also be respected. First, let us deal with space and their right to privacy. By the time a child becomes a teen, you have likely already spent years teaching him how to clean and organize his room. As children age and become teens, their rooms need to become more and more *theirs* and less ours. As with schoolwork, hygiene habits, choice in books, we must let go and allow them their decisions, mistakes and successes. As a family, you must determine family values and limits. For example, you can simply always shut their door and truly let the room be theirs. Or, if your house rules include the entire house being cleaned once a week, their room needs to be as well. The teen's room needs to be picked up so that the vacuum and dust cloth can be used and the bathroom cleaned. If the house is cleaned when they are at school, they are required to have everything picked up before they leave for school so that whoever cleans can do their job, which does not include picking up dirty clothes, bath towels, books, magazines, etc. If a room isn't ready for cleaning, the teen involved has to do the cleaning himself after school. His choice is clear: pick up and someone else cleans, fail to pick up and you clean. Or if they are involved in the cleaning process, a useful tool is: "When you have done your assigned cleaning, then you may go on with your life." Either way the room is clean by late afternoon and before the teen involved leaves the house for the evening. The rest of the time, close their door; you don't want to know. Do not let the room "talk" to you.

Every teen should have some space that she can call her own, to where she can retreat, where she can decorate to her, not our, tastes, where she can get away from others for a time, a place she calls home. This issue must not center on your paying the mortgage. Please note, it is not healthy for a teen to retreat to her room from the time she arrives home from school through bedtime. Nor should teens generally have computers or televisions in their rooms. It is far easier to supervise a computer or television in a general area of the house, a den or family room, than in a teen's bedroom. With the Internet and cable, all children need supervision. Computers, video games and television can entertain children for long lengths of time and prevent them from interacting with peers and family and from developing important communication and social skills. Help make these technological wonders a shared activity, and a supervised one, by placing them in a group area. Teens need space not total isolation. They also need supervision. Be aware of how much time they are left alone—while you are home and when you are not, even if you are working. Teens are more independent than young children; they are also more creative and capable of deception.

Respecting their time simply means that we need to understand that their time is as valuable to them as our time is to us. Infringe only when necessary and, as often as possible, as a polite request. "It would be helpful ..." and "I know it is an intrusion, but would you mind ..." both work wonders with teens. Giving them a range of time to get something done also helps. In the morning, tell them, "Sometime before four o'clock, you need to finish the last two loads of laundry." One of my friends reports that this works well with her daughter but that she has to say four o'clock *which day*. Teens are so clever.

Remembering and respecting their rapid-paced growth, change, and development are also helpful. Quite frankly, I had trouble keeping up with my sons' maturation and growing levels of knowledge, skills and understanding. They were kind enough to remind me, usually gently, but not always. Each of us remembers being treated like a child when we were teens. Try not to be one of those grownups who has forgotten what teen life is like and how easy it is to slip backwards in our treatment of an adolescent. At 19 and

21 years of age, both my sons now have a number of skills I do not, have knowledge I missed somehow, and wisdom and understanding that still take me by surprise. They are perfectly and frequently capable of helping me. I really must catch up.

Lastly, please respect and understand their vulnerability. Being a teen is not easy; it is for some of us the most difficult and most pain-filled time of our lives. We are less confident, less certain of whom we are (and will be), less developed, more filled with insecurities (acne is real), and more painfully aware of our short-comings (everyone else is cool) than at any other time in our life. Who among you would go back to age 13 willingly? I have yet to meet anyone. It is too tough. Teens are not only tough on us grownups; they are tough on themselves. Teens still need hugs, just generally not when anyone else might see. This does get better. When I whispered to Tim, then a college sophomore, that he did not have to hug me in front of his rugby team, he responded, "Mom, how old do you think I am?" and hugged me.

Chapter Checkpoints
✔   Respect them.
✔   Respect their need to be themselves and their right to be different from you.
✔   Respect their ideas.
✔   Respect their need to make decisions and their right to mess up their lives short term.
✔   Respect their space and time.
✔   Respect their growth, change and development.
✔   Respect their vulnerability and the difficulty of the "hormonally challenged" years.

Chapter 5:
Job Description

Teen Comments

"Treat your kids fairly and make them do things—fun things—together sometimes. Don't let them be ugly to each other and ignore it. Lots of kids at school don't care about their brothers and sisters and never call or talk to them. And yet, when the ones with young brothers and sisters in the family have a visit, these little kids are so happy to see their big sister or brother. What a loss not to like your brother or sister. Who else is going to be your ally in the family?"
—Kris, 20   Siblings are your best link to the past. Only they not only know but share your history.

All children and teens need to be taught their job descriptions as siblings, members of families, and as human beings. A family job description involves learning what is required of you within the family. Job descriptions simply tell us what it is we are supposed to do, what skills we must have or develop, what expectations are made of us. Keeping job descriptions to a minimum is helpful; we will keep it to six points.

Work With not Against Others

The first job description a family member has to learn is that in healthy families, people work *with* not *against* others. Modeling how we ourselves handle difficult situations and people will be our best teaching tool. We, of course, need to watch ourselves. We often work inadvertently against others, including our spouses and children. We fail to see or consider their viewpoint and their needs; we see only our own. This means that our attitude when we approach problem solving must be that together we can, and will, find a mutually agreeable solution for everyone. We will help each other and consider everyone's best interests. It means that we will ensure that we not only have, but also demonstrate, respect for another's position, ideas, and needs. Problem solving is not an opportunity to go after each other, bring up old debts, and get even. Problems offer us an opportunity to be helpful, kind and resourceful—to work with each other.

Working with, rather than against, others also includes non-problematic times. Whenever an opportunity presents itself, we need to choose to help or enhance rather than to interfere with or inhibit the situation. If you don't need your car tonight, offer it to your sister to use. If you do need it, offer to drop her off or to pick her up. If you are getting yourself a fork, why not get a fork for everyone? You can choose to make life more difficult or you can choose to make life easier for others.

Maintain or Elevate Other's Self-esteem

Teach your children that it is their job to make their sister or brother feel at least the same or better after their dealings and interactions with them. Teach your children that there are already enough insensitive and hurtful people in the world and enough painful situations. We have no need to add to this.

When you hurt with words or hands, you will need to make amends, and part of the making of amends must include helping to make the person you caused pain to feel better. Sometimes this entails doing something for them, reconsidering and changing our actions, making sure we understand their point of view, somehow undoing what we have done. For example, if one sister tells another that she has no style, the first sister may need to share expertise, clothes, magazines, and ideas with the hurt sister if she, the injured party, is open to this. Or the hurtful sister may need to accede that actually her sister does have style, it is just different from her own.

The world will tell us what is wrong with us. Our family should help us see what is right, or at the very least, gently help us learn to improve things *we choose to change.*

Contribute to the Level of Good Will—Get Along!

Margaret Anderson, in her book, *Raising a Family is a Pleasure*[7] phrases it this way: "Teach your children that

life is too short for disagreeableness for it destroys
happiness. When one must disagree with others, do it
agreeably." How very insightful and wise. In other words,
their job is to get along. Perhaps we could just teach "be
nice." But that is not enough: we have to teach them how to
get along with social skills, graces, and respectful
communication when there is no dispute. We will have to
show them how to be helpful and get along when there is
dispute by using problem solving, paradigm shift[8] and
negotiation skills. Clearly, teaching excellent problem-
solving skills[9] *as problems arise* is necessary and beneficial.
As well, we will need to demonstrate getting along and
disagreeing agreeably, not only within the family, but also
out in the real world. When someone cuts in front of us in
the checkout line at the grocery store, how good are our
skills? When children quarrel or get ugly to each other, sit
them down and remind them of their job description. Then,
teach them how to solve problems agreeably. By the time
they are teens, they will have excellent life skills.

Support and Protect[10]

As I watched my sons grow up, I witnessed a fair
amount of fighting between them, both physical and verbal.
It therefore amazed me the first time I saw a neighbor go
after my younger son and observed his older brother come to
his aid. This no longer surprises me, but I still marvel at one
brother coming to the aid of the other. Recently, less than an
hour after I had failed to listen to one son (in Austin), and as

a result over-helped with his life, his brother (in Los Angeles) called me. Ever so gently, and even wisely, Kris suggested to me (in Dallas-Fort Worth) that not only had I blown it with Tim, but I had done so by missing Tim's perspective entirely. Kris, who knows me well, suggested that by being lost in my own frustrations, I had passed my bad day on to Tim. Kris was right. He was also looking after his brother. Yes, I called and apologized and took time to consider where Tim was coming from; his brother had already made this clear for me. And yes, he had a good point that I had missed. This whole process was made much easier and smoother by one brother's support of another. I wish that family communication could always work this well.

The point is that brothers and sisters look after each other always, but especially in bumpy or rough times. In extreme situations, brothers and sisters protect each other, from others or from themselves. They do whatever is necessary. This is why kids need to tell when siblings are using drugs or driving recklessly, but do not tell when they sneak to a movie they are not supposed to see or get into minor trouble at school. Not telling on each other seems to be a universal "Teen Code" of behavior. Don't put your children into the position of telling on their siblings and violating their sibling's trust unless the issue is very important—life altering or life threatening. Did you tell on your brothers and sisters? I have so much dirt on my brother, I could put him away for years, or at the very least get him cut out of the will. Of course, he has the same amount on me. I don't think we will ever be telling.

This looking out for each other is also important among all family members. A mother who had lost a teenage son to suicide was asked what piece of advice she wanted to give to parents. She paused for a moment and then in a strained voice said she would tell parents to *be there* for their kids. She would tell them that family was supposed to be a haven for kids, and that, in this world, kids need a haven. She added that many women her age appear lost in their own world and problems. We need to remember to focus not only on ourselves; we need to be there for our kids. This is our job.

As children age, they begin to offer support and protection to us. It is a comfortable feeling to know that if anything should ever happen to their father, my sons would be there for me. White knights are a nice thing to have in reserve. Our sons both attend the same university; that, too, though unexpected is comforting. I know they look out for each other even when they are apart; this is made easier when they are close together. They are quite simply—brothers. Perhaps a brother was our best gift to each of them.

Do the RIGHT Thing: Build Character

Mary Pipher, in *The Shelter of Each Other:*

Rebuilding Our Families,[11] defines character "as that within a person which governs moral choices ... it is teaching the young to make wise and kind choices." Pipher declares that when our society lost track of character and focused on self-esteem alone, we made a mistake. I agree. As she goes on to say:

> Many clients are more worried about their children's feelings than their behavior and they focus more on their self-esteem than their character. They want their children to be happy more than they want them to be good. It's understandable that parents feel this way, but it's misguided. Happiness ultimately comes from a sense that one is contributing to the well-being of the community. In reality, making wise moral choices is the most direct route to true happiness.

When did we stop teaching children that it was important to do the right thing? For it certainly seems as though we have. (Perhaps when we started rewarding them for good behavior and paying them to be good, we lost our focus on doing the right thing just because it is the right thing.) How is it that so many of us seem to have stopped teaching this very important lesson? Did we lose the understanding that self-esteem is a *result* of good choices, not just a cause or source of them? Living our values is the surest route to having our children accept them as their own. We must teach children that choosing to do the right thing, generally the harder option, makes one feel better about oneself, allows one to feel right, and is part of one's job description as a sibling, and as a member of our larger human family.

Choosing to live by the virtues of honesty, generosity, justice, self-control, dependability, kindness, impartiality, diligence, to name only a few, builds self-esteem and self-regard. Giving in to temptations, or choosing the easy way, is often the less than honest or moral way. It involves the vices of pride, dishonesty, laziness, malice, greed, wrath, and gluttony. Generally, these make us feel good only for a moment, then inevitably make us feel worse about ourselves over the long run.

It is clear then that we must teach our children to make good choices, those which are moral, prudent and kind. We must ask them how they feel when they have chosen wisely, and also when they have chosen unwisely. Helping teens to see the difference between short-term "highs" and long-term real gains in self-regard is critical. Our most powerful teaching tool is, again, modeling, by making good decisions and practicing the virtues we espouse. This is easier said than done, but very important. We have again returned to our idea of integrity. In addition, the simple and frequent opportunities for discussion, as they arise, and they will, especially at the family dinner table, cannot be overrated. And if you don't sit down to dinner as a family at least four or five times a week, find a way and a time to talk with your teen on a regular basis. Sometimes we overlook that teens need our ear at least as much as and sometimes more than younger children do.

Live the Golden Rule

Everyone knows the Golden Rule: we just have difficulty applying it. This job description is summed up by the words of wisdom found in this correct principle of behavior: Do unto others as you would have them do unto you. Treat your family and friends the way you want them to treat you, and avoid treating them in ways you do not like to be treated. The question of integrity reappears here. Are you who you want to be, who you want others to perceive you as being, and who you want your sisters and brothers to be to you? Do your actions match your beliefs? Or is the Golden Rule simply a bunch of words?

Consider the possibilities when we take the time to teach each of our children to act by the Golden Rule. How much easier, calmer, and more agreeable would family life be? This lesson is worth teaching and reteaching, likely a thousand times for each child. Don't you still struggle with putting this simple wisdom into action in everyday life? I know I do. The struggle has to be worthwhile for I am not sure how well families or the world at large can function without this principle.

In conclusion, we cannot expect any child or teen to know or become proficient with any aspect of a job description unless we teach the concept. Our job description is what we are required to do as part of our position or role within a home, workplace or the world at large. We must teach and reteach the actual components of the job.

> Teach and model skills before you expect performance.

Chapter Checkpoints

✔   Work *with* not *against* others: together, we can and will get through this.

✔   Maintain and enhance the self-esteem of others.

✔   Get along. Create good will. Be nice. Life is just too short to do otherwise.

✔   Support family members, especially siblings, at all times. Learn to protect loved ones in extreme situations—even from themselves if necessary.

✔   Do the RIGHT thing. This is rarely easy, but always the best policy in the long run. You do own all of what you do—whether you want to or not.

✔   Practice the Golden Rule. Remember what goes around comes around.

Chapter 6:
LISTEN: Don't Know Your Teen
WATCH: Know Your Teen

Teen Comments

"Don't force your kids to talk, to give up all of the information you think is necessary; just let them know that they can talk to you. Given opportunities, they will talk to you. Also know what your kids are doing without interrogating them; it's easy for good kids to become bad kids if no one is watching." —Tim, 18

"I can't tell you how much I hate it when teenagers act like adults are aliens, and vice versa, and therefore can't talk to one another. Open lines of communication are very important in every possible type of relationship, and some teens are really horrible at this." —Sheila, 18 I might add, so are some adults!

"I always know when my friends' parents aren't involved in their lives. Not only are there no limitations on their social life, but they never seem to want to leave my house. I think they enjoy having someone actually interested in their thoughts." —Mary, 16

The title of this chapter might appear to be misleading or, at the very least, confusing. Both sections, "Know Your Teen" and "Don't Know Your Teen," address not making assumptions about your child. Learn to listen because you want to discover who your teen is as she develops and changes, rather than assuming you know what she thinks, feels and believes. Learn to watch because you should not assume that you know all that is going on in your teen's life. Kids, and the challenges they are facing, change. It is your job to *know* what truly is taking place. Again, there must be no assumptions on our part.

LISTEN means to listen *only*: not to listen and then to give advice; not to listen and then to judge; not to listen and then to discount their ideas; not to listen and then to preach; not to listen and to take someone else's (including your own) side; not to listen and not try to really understand or care. To just listen, without interjecting any of the unhelpful responses, can be exceedingly difficult.

One of the best tips I ever heard came from a mother who said she always continued to wonder who her adult child was and had been. She never *assumed* that she knew. She took steps to find out who her daughter was and was becoming. She said she was constantly asking herself about her daughter, "Who is she? What does she think about this? What does she believe? What is important to her? What are her needs?" This mother believed that the journey of discovery was fascinating. What fun to get to really know her daughter. How wonderful for the daughter to have no assumptions made about her.

Take Time

Time is a most precious gift. Time given in listening and in discovery is most precious. Taking time to listen to our teens talk about what *they choose to discuss* is a gift to them and to us. Don't you want to know exactly who your son or daughter is, and what he or she really thinks, believes and values? Whose opinions are more important than your child's? You certainly do not want to miss out on this. Listening is an essential discovery tool. Being available is key here. We must listen when they feel like talking. Trust me, it's rarely convenient; it's almost always important to take time to listen if for no other reason than to let them know you are interested and available when big issues arise.

Communication is a bridge which needs constant repair and upkeep. The time and energy involved prove their worth in times of crisis or stress. Let them talk when and about what they choose. At the dinner table, in the car, on the back porch or on a walk, ask them what they think and believe. Don't correct it. Listen and you will gain priceless knowledge available nowhere else.

It is critical that parents WATCH their children and learn to know them, to know whom they are with, and to know what they are doing. Although it may sound as though I am contradicting the first part of this chapter, I am not. LISTENING involves discovering what they are thinking. WATCHING means knowing what they are doing. You must know what is taking place in your teen's life. It is so easy to lose track. They are with us less than when they were young, and many become more secretive, withdrawn, introverted or simply distant as teens. They need space to grow and develop. There are lots of temptations, pitfalls, and missteps out there. Know what is going on in your teen's life.

Be Vigilant and Involved

For example, stay quiet when you drive car pool and learn more information than you want and also most of the information you need. Attend their events or volunteer at school functions. If your son has a friend he is spending most of his time with, invite that friend to dinner and get to know him. If your daughter spends much of her time in her room, visit. Find out what she is doing in there. If your teen reads a particular author's books, read one; if he plays one video game constantly, watch him play and discover what he is learning from the game. Stay tuned into and be aware of your children's activities.

Slacker Parents

Recently, there was an incident in a nearby town where seniors from one high school had the creativity and wherewithal to set up their own prom-like dance, with no school link.   Needless to say, at this teens-only, unchaperoned dance, there was alcohol. (As several teens told me, that would be much of the point of organizing their own dance.) The police discovered the teens at this dance and made them call their parents to come and get them. To the teens' credit, many had pre-organized taxi rides to avoid drinking and driving. The concern, of course, is how many parents knew about this event and what would be involved and how many did not even know it was taking place. How many parents did not tune in to the fact that their kids were quite excited for the week prior to the event, were overdressed for a regular night out, had made secretive phone calls to each other about the dance? Often the signs are present, we need to tune in and see them. We also need to act on them.

Spying on your teens is not what I am suggesting here. Be up front with them about your job description as a parent.   Teach them about their track record of trust. Checking up on teens is warranted only when they give us a reason, usually by lying or drastically changing their behavior, attitude or habits. Tell teens from the beginning that you are going to check up on them after trust is broken; you do not want to break trust with them. Keeping track of them, however, is always our job. Do you remember those public service announcements on television which used to ask, "It's 11:00 p.m.; do you know where your child is?" Each of us needs to know.

One of our sons bemoaned the fact that his dad had been a high school assistant principal and knew all of the tricks and his mother wrote a book on discipline. But in the next breath, he revealed that if he had had what he labeled "slacker parents" (parents who are not involved, who do not watch, who do not seem to know or care what their children are doing), he probably would have tried selling drugs. The money was so easy, and it took so much less time and effort than working his hourly wage job. The temptation, he said, was great. He wouldn't have sold any really hard drugs, just marijuana. (We all have our limits.) "High school drug dealers selling only at school rarely get shot, generally don't serve time for their first offense, and mostly don't get caught," he reasoned. They just make good money providing a product already in good supply. The risks were minimal, and the benefits were great—in his mind. I will always be glad my husband and I were not slacker parents. We could have lost a good kid.

> Even good kids sometimes make poor choices. So do good adults.

In the aftermath of the Columbine High School murders in Colorado in 1999, many people have asked how two teenagers could have had the time and isolation to build bombs in the family garage. If your teen is spending a good deal of time alone and isolated, it's time to take food out to the garage (if that's the place) and ask her what she's doing.

Are they involved in a school project? What is it? Tell me about what is going on at school. An isolated teen is an abandoned teen; we all have a responsibility to include our children in our daily lives. Apart from that, allow them a healthy distance, and privacy, in which they can practice who they are.

None of us can afford to be a slacker parent. Teens continue to need us involved in their lives, just in a different way from when they were younger. Check up on your kids when it seems prudent. If you overdo it, you have violated their privacy. If you under do it, you have denied them the right to receive prudent parenting. This may not be an easy line to find, but it is an important one.

Chapter Checkpoints
✔ Do not make assumptions about your teen. You may be wrong. Worse still, you may never even know you are wrong.
✔ The more you listen, the more you will know. Don't miss the wonder of discovering who this blossoming adult is.
✔ Prudent watching is part of a parent's job description. Temptation will beckon: be a buffer. Until a teen is strong enough to say, "No, that's wrong; I'm not interested," it is a good middle step to be able to say, "I can't; I'll get caught," or "I can't; my parents will be worried, concerned, or disappointed."

Chapter 7:
Follow Through:
Don't Start What You Can't Finish!

Teen Comments

"Anyone can make threats or empty promises. Following through reconfirms credibility. If a parent does not follow through in discipline, a kid has no reason to believe she can share her thoughts and feelings without having them revealed." —Heather, 20

"Doing what you say you will help anyone trust you." —Kris, 20

"Knowing what lines not to cross, sets up an uncrossable line of respect that cuts back on manipulation and arguments." —Courtney, 18

It is now time to talk about discipline. Two ingredients must be present in all true disciplinary actions. The first, respect, was discussed in Chapter 4. Don't overlook the fact that respect is a component of good discipline: whenever you violate another's dignity, you create resistance, power struggles, ill will and rebellion. Recognize your contribution to these and avoid them as much as possible. The second ingredient, on which this chapter focuses is authority; it is a huge factor in the effectiveness and ease of discipline.

Every parent must establish and maintain authority; hopefully you established your authority while your children were young because authority is much easier to establish with young children. However, it is never to late to start. But what is meant by authority? It is the ability to mean what you say without getting ugly and to follow through with what you said you were going to do. In other words, what you start, you finish. When a child or teen believes this, because you have proven it to him repeatedly by doing what you said you would, discipline is easier.

Don't Start What You Can't Finish
Authority is essential to being effective. Discipline without authority tends to be ineffective. Just as we cannot afford to be ugly because we undermine our relationship, similarly, we cannot afford to be nice but ineffective. "Don't start what you can't finish!" is an important lesson to learn for maintaining our authority. To be effective in discipline, it is critical that we are able to consistently follow through with three steps to maintaining authority:

    1. Say what you mean respectfully.

    2. Mean what you say and remember what you started.

    3. Take the action stated when necessary.

Whenever we do not follow through and finish the discipline we have started, we teach children to test us. Teens are great testers of authority. This is neither good for us nor any fun at all.

Please note, it is not being suggested that it is necessary to discipline every incident, every misbehavior. I am suggesting that we must follow through with what we start. Choose your battles wisely. Once we have chosen to start discipline but have not followed through, we have not done what we said we would. In doing this, we overlook that we have lied to the child and broken trust. Our word is not good; we cannot be trusted; our track record of trust is violated. This can be damaging to any relationship. Distrust is toxic to relationships and returns to haunt us, especially when our children begin to believe it is not necessary for them to be trustworthy.

It seems that more and more parents report that they have difficulty following through. They start out saying, "No, you can't stay out any later," and end up allowing the teen another hour or two. They say, "No phone calls until your homework is finished. Then they give their teen permission to talk with a friend for "just a few minutes." Over-indulging our children because we are too weak or too weary to follow through is very unhelpful to our children. It threatens both our relationship with them and our ability to be effective.

I am privileged to have a friend who has three children older than my own. Everyone needs an experienced parent as a friend. Diane's daughter wanted to spend the night with four girlfriends on a houseboat out on a nearby lake. Diane and her husband decided not to allow her to do so. It turned out that three of Ashley's friends were also told no by their parents. Interestingly, two of those three did spend the night on the boat, and then were promptly grounded the next day when they returned home. Of course, to the girls, staying overnight on the houseboat was well worth the price of grounding.

I asked Ashley if she had been tempted to go. When she replied that she had, I asked why she hadn't just gone anyway and paid the price later like her friends. Ever so gently, she gave me that just-how-stupid-are-you look and then kindly helped me out with, "Madelyn, you know my parents." I asked her what she meant. She said that she was to be in by midnight that night. Because Ashley has to call if she is going to be late, her parents would realize by 12:15 a.m. that she was missing and not coming home. By 12:20 a.m., they would be on their way to the lake to get her. By 1:00 a.m., Ashley knew she would be home in her own bed. She said there was no point in going; they would come and get her. (This is a Texas technique we like to call "Go Fetch.") What Ashley's parents had taught her earlier was that if they say something, they mean it, and it is going to happen. If they say she cannot spend the night on the houseboat, she will not be doing so, *even if they have to inconvenience themselves.* They follow through. Because Ashley believes they do, they did not have to go fetch her. She came home herself. This is authority, or "don't start what you can't finish," at work. Once a child or teen believes in our authority, our determination to follow through, she can stop testing because it's futile and foolish to do so. Discipline without authority is rarely effective. It is imperative that you have authority; without it, you risk being overrun by your teen.

Believe in Yourself

Our own belief in ourselves and the importance of our job as parents is key to carrying authority. A full understanding of our job description with regard to discipline is essential. Our job description: *when our child or teen invites us into his life with irresponsibility or misbehavior, we accept the invitation and arrive in their lives directly.*

Concern

The ability to turn anger or fear into concern for our child's welfare also affects our level of authority. When we truly love someone, it means we are willing to put their best interests first. No small task, but again an important key to parenting.

Keys to Authority[12]

O—ᴊ **"Don't start what you can't finish."** Always follow through with what you started. Remember: choose your battles wisely.

O—ᴊ **Believe in yourself.** Our body language, including our tone of voice, reflects directly how much we believe in what we are saying and how important it is. It is critical that we are sure of what we say and how we say it. With correct principles and life lessons guiding us, we can be certain.

O—ᴊ **Concern.** Concern for another's welfare and well-being is far more powerful and helpful than anger.

Chapter Checkpoints
✔ Say what you mean: stop and think before you speak.
✔ Mean what you say: remember and watch.
✔ Follow through: do what you said you would. Build trust and authority.
✔ Believe in yourself. Know your job description and follow it.
✔ Turn anger and fear into concern. Discipline is always about *their* best interests.

Chapter 8:
Live Your Principles

Teen Comments

"I was raised to have strong moral values. It is confusing and defeating, however, to discover that the ones who taught you such convictions do not practice them. It's like a nun lecturing on kindness and then witnessing her cruelty to others." —Heather, 20

"Some of the harder times in my life have been from watching hypocritical actions come from my parents. These actions knock off a huge center of knowledge and morality in my head and test their authority." —Courtney, 18 I wonder who of us hasn't violated our own integrity along the way?

Develop Character by Example

Good teens do exist. There are more of them than the media would have us think. Most teens, like most adults, do the job that life demands of them and without great crises. As we grownups perform the jobs demanded by our lives, we are being watched by our children. We all learn what we witness. Teens act in ways they have seen the significant adults in their lives behave. "Do as I say, not as I do" has never proven itself to be a useful policy or suggestion. It has always been true that modeling, how we act, what we choose to do, is our strongest teaching tool. Sadly, it is not easy to practice what we preach and behave as we believe everyone should. For example, let's assume that each of us believes in The Golden Rule, "Do unto others as you would have them do unto you." We recognize this rule for the correct principle that it so simply states. However, it is likely that each of us struggles with putting The Golden Rule into practice every day of our lives. When we miss, we are likely witnessed by our children.

Here are some examples: our teens watch our drinking habits. If we choose to drink, do we handle alcohol well or do we abuse it? Do we always follow the letter of the law? Do you have a drink and then drive? Young people watch our dating patterns if we are single, and they learn the truth of what we really believe about sex outside of marriage. They watch the way we treat other people, other races, other people's property. Are we respectful? Do we have prejudices? Children see our biases even when we are blindly unaware of them ourselves. When our teen says, "Well, you do it!" he always has a point. Each of us needs to have a healthy fear of hearing these few incisive words.

Good teens come into being where and when they have been given opportunities to develop character, they have been taught excellent life lessons, and they have had excellent examples set, reset, and set again. We parents don't just get to be good once. This section speaks to watching and governing our own behavior. This is at times challenging and uncomfortable. But if we are to help our teens develop character and the ability to make prudent choices, we must become aware of the effect our behavior has not just on ourselves but on our children.

Teach Values & Virtues

As parents we must teach our children both values and virtues. Parents can teach both; educators can teach only virtues. (One exception is when you teach in a private church-affiliated school, you may teach the church's religious beliefs as parents have agreed to, indeed sought, these values to be included in their child's educational process.) Values are positive or negative stances we take or hold toward issues. As a large and diverse population, we disagree on values, which include such concepts as if God exists and in what form, whether or not to have premarital sex, whether or not to drink, whether or not abortion is appropriate, whether or not reading books is important, etc. We do not have consensus. As a parent, I do not want teachers using their classroom to teach my child their values, or positions on issues, by promoting their values as right. Teaching values is *my* job. My values are the ones that I want taught to my child. They are called *family values* for an excellent reason.

Each of us "teaches" values by modeling our own personal choices of behavior; this is unavoidable and happens around us all the time. Our children are witness to this daily. By the time children are teens, they will have watched their parents' behavior for their lifetime. As well, if you have spent enough time at dinner, at bedtime, on walks, during times of crisis or decision-making, discussing your own family values, your message and values will be imprinted on their minds.

Do not be afraid of teens discussing values with their peers. As children age into late adolescence, it becomes their job to question almost everything, including their parents' values. We want our teens to be able to think and question. Independent thinking need not be feared. Our children need to think for themselves and to discover and embrace what is right for them. They are not stupid; they can and do figure out things for themselves. We, their parents, give them the tools, the background information, the articulated thoughts, and the shared experiences to be able to sort through this difficult but exciting task. Don't worry. Interestingly enough, most children end up with values fairly close to what their parents lived. Hopefully what you live and tell them coincide.

Virtues are another thing entirely. Both educators and parents need to teach these. Virtues are skills—not opinions—by which we conduct our lives, and which make our lives, and the lives of others, better. They include characteristics such as prudence, fortitude, moderation, and justice. Loyalty, honesty, gratitude, dependability, self-reliance, agreeableness, impartiality, friendliness, generosity, thoughtfulness, self-control, and humility are also virtues. We all recognize that adding any of these to our life enhances it. Even as a diverse society, we do not disagree on the benefits of virtues.

Although it is true that virtues are more easily taught to the young, and reinforced as habits, it is never too late to learn virtues. Our job is two-fold. It appears that these days we must teach our children what virtues are; we must label them when we see them or witness their absence. Secondly, we need to help them see the outcomes of virtuous versus non-virtuous behavior. For example, when they persevere and work hard and as a result, finish a job or get the higher grade, it is helpful to point out to them both their fortitude and its benefits. When they choose not to persevere, we must also help them see this outcome along with its cause. When they are dependable, others trust them; when they demonstrate self-reliance, they feel good about themselves and things get done or problems get solved; when they are generous with their time, spirit or objects, others benefit greatly, and the world is a better place.

Always when we choose virtue, we feel right about ourselves in the long term; we enhance our self-regard.

When we choose other than virtue, we may feel good for a moment, but over the long term we lose. The goal is to feel right not good. We can lie and make others believe we are something we are not, and look and feel good for a moment. But generally, the lie returns to haunt us, and we are discovered for what we truly are. Rejection, derision, or avoidance usually follow. Most importantly, we can end up feeling wrong. And that is as it should be. Feeling awful, with its accompanying development of conscience and character, helps us to choose never to make the same mistake again. High self-esteem, seeing ourselves honestly, and feeling right about ourselves, come from making the right (virtuous) behavioral decisions. Teach your children virtues. Model virtues. Virtues haven't changed since time began; they are not likely to in our lifetime.

> Act right, feel right. Act wrong, feel wrong.

Chapter Checkpoints
✔   What you say is heard.
✔   What you do is seen.
✔   "Do as I say, not as I do" has always failed as a teaching tool.

Chapter 9:
Sense of Humor

Teen Comments

"Humor has a way of bringing us back together after we have had an argument." —Garrett, 16

"The serious talks drain me and the fights frustrate me, but the laughter is what I walk away remembering." —Courtney, 18

He who laughs at himself will never cease to be amused. —Anonymous

Having and using a sense of humor is for many parents of teens what gets them through these years. Humor is the grease that lubricates the wheels of the family and allows it to move ahead more smoothly in bumpy times.

Humor is a wonderful way to change moods, meld as a family, and get through troubled times. In most families, we would be lost and life would be uglier without a fairly constant stream of humor. When things begin to get ugly, and they sometimes do, reach for humor. Children and teens almost always respond positively; so, too, do adults. It is important to keep the humor within the child's level; it is easy to go over a child's head. It is easy to alienate teens with humor if there is even a hint of making fun of, or laughing at, them. Always avoid sarcasm, derision, mockery, belittling, and ridicule—anything which brings down another person. Using humor consists of fun with them, not fun at their expense. Teen self-confidence tends to run low. Although they often pressure others to be hardy, the truth is that their skin is not thick and hurt can happen easily. Teens can be volatile and easily upset; go gently with your choice of humor.

Successful humor is aided by our strong interpersonal bonds. Having previously established a sense of trust and safety allows me a freer range of humor. Don't let yourself miss out on humor with teens: it can be pretty outrageous. When our older son went to college, he phoned from the University of Texas and boldly stated that I needn't worry because there was no beer in Austin. (A college town without beer? I'm old, but not that old.) When I then asked whether there were any girls (another temptation) in Austin, he quickly replied, "Only virgins, Mom." How can I not love this kid? He eased my stress with humor. If you like someone, it is easy to find them funny; when you don't like someone, humor can sound pretty lame. Conversely, humor can help to strengthen an already-present bond.

Another important skill or lesson we can model for our children is the ability to laugh at ourselves, not to take life so seriously. Frankly and fortunately, few of the things in life we must deal with are life-threatening. Humor is especially helpful when the chips are down or we are looking bad in any way. Humor is one of the best tools I know for tough times. It has been used extraordinarily well at funerals, in hospital rooms, in times of deep sorrow, great fear and major stress, as well as during the easier times such as when your teen's report card is not what had been hoped for, or when your teen is involved in a minor accident, or even when her haircut is a bad one. That last one, the bad haircut, is an excellent example of where one can go wrong. If you make fun of the haircut ("You look like Don King,") rather than the situation ("The difference between a good haircut and a bad one is about four weeks,") your teen is most likely to burst into tears. Use humor first, to ease mood and stress; then go to problem solving.

A day without humor is like a day without sunshine —just too dark.

Chapter Checkpoints

✔   A sense of humor is essential to easing the way through stress, fear, confusion, sorrow—all of the dark times. It is a wonderful addition to any day.

✔   Change moods first, then minds.

✔   Humor must NEVER be at the expense of the teen; not only will this blow up in your face and change the mood for the worse, but it will also damage the bond between the two of you. Be very careful.

✔   Be gentle and respectful with your humor. The job of humor is to ease, not provoke, a situation.

Chapter 10:
Essential Techniques

Teen Comments

"Learning to take responsibility for myself and my actions was one of my most difficult lessons, but one of the most important." —Heather, 20

What are some techniques we can effectively use with teens to maintain our relationship, encourage mutual respect, and establish authority? How do we effectively communicate and discipline? How do we maintain our own credibility and integrity? How do we ensure they are not just ready, but well-prepared, to leave the nest? Finally, how do we lay the foundation for a long-term, strong, and healthy relationship with our children when they become adults?

Disciplinary Consequences[13]

A powerful technique, disciplinary consequences, is a remarkable method for teaching teens to make good decisions by looking ahead to outcomes. They must learn to think about what could possibly happen, what the outcome might be, if they choose a particular behavior, rather than simply thinking about and choosing between behavior options. For example, they must learn to think ahead to whether they want to fail a test or pass it (outcome) rather than simply deciding whether they want to study for the test or not (behavior).

Allowing young people to experience consequences as a disciplinary tool continues to be misunderstood and misused. A consequence, by definition, can be anything that follows an event or an action. This could conceivably include rewards and punishments, neither of which is a form of discipline.[14] Thus, we will use the term DISCIPLINARY CONSEQUENCE to focus our concept of consequences to disciplinary actions only. Please note: the consequences included here will always be *fair, reasonable, direct, and related to the action preceding them.* This type of disciplinary consequence will also always *teach* the child a lesson he requires at the time. Consequences also teach ownership, not only of behavior, but more importantly, of the results and effects of the behavior. Disciplinary consequences can quite effectively teach the fundamental principle of accountability:

> You are responsible for what you choose to do and for what happens to you and others as a result of your decisions and actions.

Disciplinary consequences are frequently and mistakenly confused with punishments and rewards. These systems of behavior management, which are not recommended, use the word *consequence* to describe punishments: a demerit or detention for misbehavior at school, phone privileges removed for being late, the loss of any unrelated privilege. They also use the term consequence to describe rewards: stickers for the young, a car for good grades, a monetary reward for any positive behavior, or any unrelated privilege given for any good behavior. Making a child pay or rewarding a child are distinctly different from allowing a child to experience the related or naturally occurring consequences of her behavior. The use of the term "consequence" in this text is strictly limited to actions which are related to a specific antecedent behavior, not simply any action taken after the fact. Disciplinary consequences always teach a lesson concerning the specific mistake or misbehavior; they clearly link behaviors and outcomes. They are never arbitrary or spiteful.[15]

Here are some examples. Since your teen started school this year, she has been constantly on the phone with her friends from the time she arrives home from school until the time she goes to bed. Last year she hardly used the phone at all. Her first grading period report card shows that her grades have slipped significantly. Discussing the concern with her, you learn that her grades dropped due to incomplete homework, something which has arisen from her time on the telephone. The related consequence is to remove phone privileges until all homework is finished or to limit phone use to a specific number of minutes (say fifteen) per evening. Taking away television privileges or grounding her for three weekends would be neither fair nor linked and would constitute punishment, not discipline. Offering her money or a new CD player if she gets better grades is a reward or bribe, again unrelated and not discipline. Further, neither the punishment nor the bribe solves the problem.

If her time on the phone is not the cause of the lowered grades, rather the problem is her not knowing what homework she has each night, removing phone privileges will not help. Getting a daybook or an assignment notebook and learning how to use it would be the better solution, the better disciplinary action.

When any teen earns his driver's license, it is critical to tell him the following: "Should you get a traffic ticket for unsafe driving (not for a parking violation or late license renewal violation which are not life-threatening), you need to know that no judge will be necessary for the removal and loss of your license. I will take it—for two reasons: first, you do not have the right to risk the lives of others. Period. Second, you do not have the right to risk the life of the most precious person on the planet, you. As your parent, I will protect you from anything or anyone, including yourself, who places you in danger." This is not about you, the parent or your power or what you can take away from your teen. It is about rights and losing them. It is about what will happen if this teen exercises poor judgment in a car. If a teen abuses this privilege by driving unsafely, he will lose the privilege of using a car and our roads. If, on the other hand, the teen handles the car responsibly, then he will keep this privilege and responsibility.

Chapter One dealt with freedom and responsibility and demonstrated the link between the two. There will be many opportunities to use disciplinary consequences to teach this connection. Parents who, after a safety violation, buy a teen a second car, or continue to pay insurance, or allow a teen to drive after this safety violation (speeding, running a red light, driving while intoxicated) have made a grave mistake. Either they are not strong enough to make safety a priority, or they do not understand that love means putting their children's best interests first. Perhaps some are simply too busy to be inconvenienced to discipline their children, or are too isolated from their children and their job as parents to deal with the problem. Without question, it is troublesome to lose that new, extra driver (of himself, of his siblings, for errands); it is painful beyond description to lose a child. Inconvenience yourself. Inconvenience your teen. As difficult as this is, teach this lesson the "easy" way, the first time.

Here are additional examples of disciplinary consequences: 1)Ground your child only when freedom to roam has been violated by staying out past curfew, going places other than those agreed upon (a trust violation), or participating in inappropriate activities such as taking drugs or performing vandalism. 2)If completing chores becomes a problem, saying, "When you finish your chores, then you may go on with your life," (take or make phone calls, go to a friend's, play video games, go to practice) can prove helpful. 3)If you end up doing one of their chores, putting gas in the car after they depleted the tank, making their bed so the house can be shown by the real estate agent, making dinner on the night they are assigned, then they owe you time for time, chore for chore. They will need to do one of your chores. 4)If they fail to put gas in the car after using it, an alternative disciplinary measure is that they lose the privilege of driving the car. 5)If they do get a parking violation ticket, they pay for the ticket; however, since they have not risked life and limb, they continue to have use of the car.

At some point in time, many teens face the "ride with a friend who has been drinking" dilemma and decision. A teen who has neither experienced disciplinary consequences, nor learned to make behavioral decisions based on outcome not instant gratification, is at peril. The question this type of teen asks herself sounds like this, "Shall I go with my friends and have a good time or stay behind by myself?" She'll tell herself the following: "I'll go with my friends." If, however, experiencing and living with disciplinary consequences has taught her to ask outcome-based questions, her thought will be, "Shall I get in the car with a drunk driver or not? Is tonight a good night to risk my life?" That answer too is obvious; tonight is not a good night to die. Her decision could save her life. Later, the question may become, "Do I want to use a condom or really show him that I love him and not use one?" Or it could be, "Do I want to have sex at this point in my life? Do I want to risk getting AIDS and risk my life?" The questions our children ask themselves make all the difference in their choices.

> Teach them to consider outcomes or consequences at the same time they are considering behavior or temptation. Our children are not stupid; given the tools to ask the right questions, they make prudent decisions. This is called self-discipline. Creating this has always been the goal of our discipline.

Problem Solving

In Chapter Five, job descriptions were discussed. It was emphasized that in healthy families, family members need to work with not against each other. Needless to say, our teens will sometimes still choose to work against us or at least not with us. Problem solving is the technique most often helpful in this type of situation; it is also the *most frequently used disciplinary technique with teens.* Problem-solving skills may be the most important set of skills we ever teach our children. The most opportune time to teach problem-solving skills is when problems arise. Problems will visit our children throughout their lives; they need to know how to solve them humanely, fairly and efficiently. Learning to handle conflict respectfully and creatively is one of our most important lessons. There are six steps to problem solving.

1. Define the Problem

It is at this first step into problem solving that we often fail to sufficiently engage our children. It is crucial that we describe the problem we see from *both* our and the teen's viewpoints; when we only include our viewpoint, the teen has no reason to enter into problem solving. Furthermore, the teen is right: we want to change him and get what we want, rather than enter problem solving with no hidden agenda. Always include the child's vested interest or reason for wanting a particular problem solved. Here are some examples:

"I wonder if you feel not getting along with your brother and having him bug you are a problem?"

Instead of:

"I'm tired of you two fighting all of the time."

"I don't like having to remind you about your chores, and I bet you're tired of my nagging. Let's see if we can find a way to settle these issues of chores and nagging."

Instead of:

"You never want to do your chores. Let's find a way to work this out."

"The noise level in here is too high, and you all want to hear the television. How can we solve this problem?"

Instead of:

"We have to do something about the noise level in this room!"

Take time to listen to the teen's point of view and to her feelings about the situation. Her point of view is as important and valid as the adult's. Not taking enough time to listen can result in the child leaving or sabotaging the process, or in working on the wrong problem. Being able to switch into their paradigm, that is to say, being able to view the problem through their eyes, is very helpful here. Make sure you understand where they are coming from, how they see the problem. Their position is generally quite different from yours. You do not have to agree with them, just ensure you understand their position. Take the time to demonstrate your understanding of their viewpoint. This is a most helpful tool in reducing emotions and building real communication. Simply stated, at the very beginning, put yourself in their shoes.

After the teenager has spoken, if you feel it will be helpful to the problem solving, talk *very briefly* and *respectfully* about your viewpoint and feelings. Beware of launching into a fifteen minute dissertation on the details and correctness of your position.

Transition Phrase: "Are you ready to think about things
                        we might do to solve this problem?"

2. Brainstorm—Generate Ideas

Invite the teen to work on finding solutions. Someone who has been involved from the first step, identifying the problem, and who has helped generate solutions is far more likely to follow through with the agreed upon solution than someone who has not been involved.

It is important not to pass any judgments or make any criticism during brainstorming. Judgments stop the generation of ideas. All ideas need to be accepted for the time being. Sometimes it is helpful to write down all of the ideas at this stage. Be warned, teens sometimes find this offensive. Remember, you are not looking for the single best option; here you are simply looking for ideas, so be as creative as possible.

Transition Phrase: "Do you feel we have enough ideas
                        to begin evaluating them?"

3. Evaluate Options

Now it is time to evaluate the ideas—after several have been generated. Together, decide which ideas or portions of ideas you all feel comfortable with and which you do not like. Discuss the ideas you like best. Take time to make improvements on these promising ideas. Look for your shared interests and mutual gain; they are there. Now is the time to modify, amend or mix ideas. Be careful to avoid put-downs.

Try using:

> "I wouldn't be comfortable with that." or "I can live with this one."

Instead of:

> "This one is dumb."

Transition Phrase: "Do any of the solutions stand out as the best choice?"

4. Select the Solution That Meets Everyone's Needs

When we select a solution that meets everyone's needs, we greatly increase the odds that everyone will follow through and comply with the decision. There is, however, a vast difference between a solution that meets everyone's needs and a compromise solution. Often, we stop at a compromise rather than seeking further to find what would be mutually agreeable. In *Getting to Yes*, Fisher and Ury[16] suggest focusing on interests rather than positions to find a solution that meets everyone's needs. They tell a story about two men quarreling in a library:

> One wants the window open and the other wants it closed. They bicker back and forth about how much to leave it open: a crack, halfway, three quarters of the way. No solution satisfies them both.

Enter the librarian. She asks one why he wants the window open: "To get some fresh air." She asks the other why he wants it closed: "To avoid the draft." After thinking a minute, she opens wide a window in the next room, bringing in fresh air without a draft.

We can learn much from this story. First, taking time to find out each other's interests helps us to define the problem more clearly and thoroughly and thus more helpfully. Clarifying the *real* problem (gaining fresh air versus avoiding a draft), rather than the problem first stated (open window versus closed window), moves us closer to a long-lasting solution. Second, if the parties involved had remained with their original positions, the best solution they would have devised would have been a compromise position (window half open), where each gains some of what he wants but each also loses some of what he wants. Because neither is truly satisfied with the solution, it is less likely to be a lasting answer. Although it is no longer being addressed, in reality, there is still a problem. Third, in order to discover individual interests, the librarian asked, "Why?" ("Why do you want the window closed?" "Why do you want the window open?") Sometimes asking, "Why not?" ("Why don't you want the window closed?" "Why don't you want the window open?") can be helpful as well. Lastly, the librarian used an important skill to create the solution; she took a moment to *think*. She invented a solution for this specific problem.

> Focus on interests, not positions, to define
> the core problem and uncover mutually
> agreeable solutions that last.

Transition Phrase: "Are you ready to plan who does
                      what by when?"

5. Make a Specific Plan

Determine what steps need to be taken to get this plan into action. Decide who will be responsible for what—specifically. Set a time frame for completion of actions. Without the specifics of who, what, and when, excellent plans may fail. Be very clear. Write it down now.

Transition Phrase: "It might be helpful to think about
                      how we'll know if our solution really
                      is working."

6. Provision for Review—Plan a Failsafe

How will you know if the solution really works and if you have been successful? Determine the critical factors to success. Agree to try the plan for a short, specific time (three days, a week, a morning), and then to evaluate progress. If the plan is not working, if all parties are not satisfied, return to the first step.

Transition Phrase: "I will check with you on Thursday."

Three additional tips for problem solving include:

1. Look after everyone's interests, even those absent. ⇨Be nice.
2. Deal fairly: no lion's share or special interests. ⇨Be fair.
3. Deal straight: no hidden agendas or deals. ⇨Be honest.

Walking our children through innumerable problems, using and teaching excellent skills, nets teens and adults who can solve problems creatively, efficiently and graciously. When we focus on interest not position, when we look for mutually agreeable solutions rather than compromised ones, when we look after everyone's interests and have no hidden agendas, we have given a most wonderful and useful gift to the teen. It is also a gift to us; rarely will we need to be involved in solving their problems, for they know how to do this themselves. This is a worthwhile investment of time and effort.

Guide to Amends

When a child or teen makes a mess, breaks or loses something belonging to another, or hurts someone, it is important to help him understand the need for repair, restoration, or restitution. Our focus too often is on what went wrong rather than on what needs to be done to fix it. It is as simple as when you break something of someone else's, it is your job to fix it or replace it. If you hurt someone, your job is to help him feel better if possible. If you lose something, find it or replace it. You do not have the right to destroy another's things, body or spirits. Teaching teens to find a remedy sounds like the following:

> "When you use my car, you do not have the right to use up all the gas. I need at least enough gas to get to work. You need to go get gas on your own before you are done with the car."

Jean Clarke in *Time-In: When Time-Out Doesn't Work*[17] thoroughly discusses making amends. She suggests five excellent guidelines for determining amends to others:

1) The amender must put forth the effort.
2) Amends should support family or classroom principles.
3) Amends should help the child become a better person.
4) The amend should be related to the problem.
5) The amend must be satisfactory to the victim.

Guide to Contribution

We begin teaching children to contribute by maintaining themselves and taking care of their own needs and business, such as getting dressed and picking up their own toys. As children get older, we add that it is also their responsibility to contribute to the family. By teaching our children how to do all household chores, we are able to send them off to college or work with adequate survival skills.

We want it to be a luxury to bring laundry home, not a necessity. We do them a disservice by not helping them learn to do chores. After all, do you want your own child to marry someone who neither knows how to do chores nor expects to do them?

We also teach them to contribute in the larger arenas of their lives. As noted previously, no matter what group we belong to: family, classroom, school, church, organization, nation, planet, we need to contribute to its general welfare and maintenance. No group can afford more taking than giving. No one has the right to be a long-term or permanent parasite; short periods of non-contribution in times of great duress and need are, of course, acceptable and expected.

Taking care of only our own life and our own problems is not enough. Each of us finds himself in need of help and contribution from others at various times. This is perhaps the best use of a *credit system*. Healthy marriages and good relationships of every kind build a surplus of contributions; one never knows when the tables may turn and the resources be needed. We need to have enough resources. Teach teens that it is their job to contribute.[18]

Describe Rather than Blame

When things go wrong, we often tend to blame or accuse our teens. "You didn't feed the dog." "You fooled around and didn't do any homework all six weeks long."

Alternatively, the technique of describing focuses on *what needs to be done*. The above charges would change to: "The dog's dish is empty. It is your chore to feed him this week." Or "You need to feed the dog; he has been waiting all day." For the second example, "Your grade point average has dropped 2½ points total from the last grading period." Or "I am concerned to see five out of six of your grades lower than in the last report." A third example concerns the teen who gets up from the table without taking care of his plate. "Your dishes go in the dishwasher when you leave the table." Or "You need to put your dishes in the dishwasher when you leave the table." Use these forms instead of less respectful communication such as, "Pick up your dishes." Or "You never remember to clear your plate." Remember our job is simply to describe what they need to do.

Be Respectful and Direct

We all recognize that communication needs to be respectful. Not all of us are aware that being direct is a factor in creating emotionally healthy communication. "Direct" neither implies nor includes "ugly." Four phrases have proven themselves helpful repeatedly in dealing with teens. Each is direct and truthful.

Make sure you try this first set: *"I could sure use your help,"* and *"I could certainly use your cooperation on this."* Why do we fail so often to ask for help or cooperation from our teens? In their younger years, children love to help;

this does not go away. It just becomes hidden. Ask for help. You will be pleasantly surprised how often teens will help. Of course, we too need to model being helpful and cooperative with them.

Another helpful phrase is: "*It is your responsibility* ...to feed the dog; ...to bring home the books you need; ...to do your homework; ...to be ready by 7:30 a.m." I do not know when we stopped telling children that they have responsibilities and what those responsibilities are, but as a nation or generation, we seem rarely to do it. Naming responsibilities teaches children and teens that they are directly responsible for doing some things, for making things happen. This phrase tells concisely about responsibility and ownership. It also makes argument very difficult. Excuses will follow inevitably. Just repeat the phrase, "It is your responsibility." We must stop being afraid to tell children what their responsibilities are. We must also be willing, and able, to hold them accountable for their actions and responsibilities. This is how teens learn to become responsible adults.

The third direct phrase carries more authority yet remains respectful: "*You do not have the right* ...to hurt others with your words or your fists; ...to disrupt others' learning; ...to drive after drinking." How does one argue with "You do not have the right to drink and drive"? There is no good argument, no acceptable excuse, no way out of this violation. If you are listening to an argument after this type of phrase, learn to remove yourself or to stop the argument with, "There is no acceptable excuse. No one has the right to drink and drive—period." Say it and mean it; your teen's life may depend on it.

This phrase clearly speaks to higher level offenses. It would be inappropriate to tell a teen that he does not have the right to leave his dishes on the table after he eats.

The fourth phrase to remember, and which carries the most authority, is reserved for major digressions: dangerous actions, hurtful behavior, not listening to discipline, or trying not to own behavior. The phrase is: *"When you ...*
I am concerned because ...
I expect...."
When a teen chooses to roll his eyes and begins to walk away during discipline, try saying in a low, calm voice: "When you choose not to listen, I am concerned, because what I have to say to you is important. I expect you to listen and learn."

Let Them Talk First

It is always prudent to let others talk first in any given situation. It is an effective method of avoiding the appearance of being uninformed at best, stupid at most. When talking with teens, this is critical. When your teen breaks curfew and is late returning home, do not start into a tirade. Let him tell his tale of woe first; it may actually be true and helpful information (they took a friend to the hospital), or humorous enough to change the mood (another parent lecturing them on needing to get home on time).

When reviewing their report cards, bite your tongue and listen. We tend to start right off evaluating and telling them how they should feel. Frequently, we are off the mark. We may tell them how very proud we are that their grade in Algebra went from a C to an A. When in reality, had we listened, they might have taken the opportunity to include the fact that their grade increase coincides with their being moved behind the smartest girl in class. Unwittingly, she shared some answers.

Do Not Give Unsolicited Advice

This is easier said than done. The skill required is called "bite your tongue."

Chapter Checkpoints
✔   Disciplinary Consequences teach accountability, ownership of behavior and outcomes, and making decisions based on outcomes not just temptation.
✔   Problem Solving is the single most useful tool to use with teens.
✔   Guide to Amends teaches teens to undo negative actions to the greatest possible degree and promotes ownership of mistakes.
✔   Contributing helps teens understand that they belong to a family and a larger community, that they are not islands alone.
✔   Describing what needs to be done keeps us respectful, is future not past oriented, and teaches rather than punishes.
✔   Respect and directness are essential keys to healthy communication. Ugly is not involved.
✔   Unasked for advice is unheard and unheeded.

Chapter 11:
Letting Go

Teen Comments
> *"To let go is to let grow."* —Kris, 20

> Each child is an adventure into a better
> life—an opportunity to change the old pattern
> and make it new. —Hubert H. Humphrey

Adolescence is a time of increasing freedoms and responsibilities for the teen; in contrast, parents must let go of what the teen takes on responsibly. Two of the best places to let go are their rooms and their appearance. Learn to close the door on the room that has now become theirs. I have never seen a study correlating how a teen picks up his room and how he takes care of his home later in life, but I would wager there is no correlation.

Some teens rebel in high school; more positively put, they separate from their parents and begin to discover who they are. This is an appropriate and necessary developmental task. In order to do this, a teen will sometimes simply stop being like her parents. Any way she can be different will do.

Later, she will refine and spend more time on defining herself as she is, as opposed to being simply "not like you." Hair and clothes are excellent points of separation and rebellion. Without these safe avenues, too often kids choose to rebel in other more dangerous arenas, such as drugs, sex or crime. Teen hairstyles have never been the same as the generation before them; they never will be. There is a reason. They very much want and need to be different from the older, decrepit, no-longer-cool generation.

Make sure you are giving your teens an allowance not related to chores. They do chores because they are part of the family—period. Similarly, they need money because they are part of the family. But more importantly, they need money, to share in the family resources, to learn how to blow it, so they can begin to learn how to spend it wisely. By the teen years, it is helpful to have worked your way up to a clothing allowance. Remember, you were going to buy them clothes anyway. Let them know how much is available to them and then do not intervene. It is their choice whether or not to buy the popular, pricey items, and they most likely will. They will have fewer pieces of clothing. This can mean they will have to do a load of laundry on Wednesday if you only do it on Saturday. They may not leave themselves enough for warmer winter boots or new sports shoes. But they will own their choices. This practice not only saves you headaches if you can let go, but achieves a great deal for them in coping on their own later on.

Once when one of my friends was in Toronto shopping with her daughter Rachel, she discovered how valuable a clothing allowance was to their relationship. In a trendy "jeans" store, Rachel tried on a variety of the latest denim fashions, asking each time which pair her mother thought was best. Since the money, and therefore the decision to spend it, were Rachel's, her mother's replies were like this: "I think I like that pair better than the last, but the decision is yours." No argument; no pain; no resentment. Later, at the cashier, the young man who had helped them, approached the mother and told her how unusual the exchange had been from his day-to-day experience. Ordinarily, he said, there were loud and angry fights, rolling eyes and refusals to pay. He said most mother-daughter shopping trips were quite unhappy ones to witness. This mother thanked him for his vote of confidence and told him that she and Rachel had a clearly understood contract. Money for clothing had been previously set; the decisions on how much or what to buy were Rachel's. What would they argue about? Indeed, they planned on a happy lunch out, a celebration of their shared time together.

Other areas in which parents need to let go and hand over to their teens include homework, chores, bedtime, getting up in the morning, time management, and social activity choices. When teens make choices that can harm them physically or morally, of course, step in and help. If all is going well, then the last two years of high school are great years in which to watch and predict how a teen will handle his first couple of years away from home. Don't you want to know before they go? The only way to know is to stand back and observe.

Remember the earlier you let something go, the sooner it is no longer an issue. The sweetest words a parent can say are, "It's up to you."

"No Questions Asked" Policy

Teens all make poor judgments at one time or another. They get into situations they never anticipated nor have any idea how to handle: a driver who is drunk, a party that is not comfortable, a date who is pressing. For your teen's safety, let them know that you are always there to help, that they can always call you no matter what. Tell your teens that they can call you and ask you to come and get them from anyplace, even forbidden ones, at any time, even after curfew. Promise to ask no questions. Believe me, you will most likely hear the story directly. This offer can prevent one of your children from being stuck in an unsafe or disreputable situation. It is a truly necessary fail-safe.

A nineteen-year-old recently advised a parent education group to have exactly this policy. She explained that she had known many friends who, when in a difficult situation, like being stuck with a drunken boyfriend planning on driving home, or being uncomfortable with the level of energy or behavior (code words for drugs) at a party, had no one to turn to but other teens. Their parents, they believed, could not handle the truth, would not want to know the truth, and would make the need for help an opportunity to criticize, humiliate or even punish. She believed that her own parents' policy of No Questions Asked had not only given her an out when she needed it, but had often given her the confidence to feel she needn't rebel. Her parents truly loved her unconditionally; her safety was of the utmost importance.

When this well-meaning group of moms disagreed, saying that their child shouldn't be there in the first place, this wise teen's response was, "But what if they are? Which is more important to you—being right, or making sure they're safe?" We all must make this determination. It seems to me to be one of the easier choices we parents make with regard to bringing up our teens. I want my child alive and well. Even good teens make poor judgments; I did. When my children need a white knight, I'd like to be there for them. White knights historically rescue and hug, rather than lecture, berate, or question how one got oneself into such a mess.

Work With not Against Them

In healthy families, as in any healthy relationship or organization, people work with each other not against each other. This was noted as a job description to be taught to teens; it is also a necessary aspect of a parent's job. The more you can avoid an us versus them approach, the easier your relationship will be. Always we must strive to put another's best interest first; that is what people who love and care about each other do. Teach your kids this by practicing it. You may even be the recipient of the philosophy and practice yourself.

Intuition & Gut Feelings

Finally, listen to your own intuition and gut feelings. If you think something is wrong or not going well with your teen, you are probably right. If a story, explanation or situation feels wrong, it very likely is not fully right. If you think you are being taken for a ride, put on the brakes. If your guts tell you your child is ready for a new freedom or responsibility, that things are alright with a particular situation or friend, that you have the whole story, you are also probably right.

Intuition, for many, takes time to develop. One mother reports that although her teens sometimes touched a note within her, she did not always catch on right away. This, she relates, made her the "Master of Hindsight Education"[19]; sometimes this will be our method of learning. Still, no one has a greater opportunity to know your child than you do. Take advantage.

Conclusion

The bottom line is this: the teen years will bring

some new and interesting challenges. We knew when our children first walked that there would be missteps and bumps and bruises along the way. We learned there were places where we needed to put up gates and safety hinges, and we learned that there were many times that there was little else we could do but pick them up and comfort them.

Similarly, our teens need our support and encouragement as they explore the large world they will soon inhabit. They need to be given an opportunity to take clear steps towards independence. They need to be both forgiven and understood as we encourage them to make forays out and away from family and to achieve some separation. This is not so unlike your toddler clinging to your leg, then taking steps into the sandbox to his playmates, playing happily for a time, and then returning into our arms after this dizzying but exhilarating foray into new frontiers. They must, through the teen years, begin to emerge as people with their own distinct identities and value systems. They must learn to be responsible for their own needs, feelings and behaviors. We will not always be able to pick them up and make everything all better; they must learn to do this for themselves. And finally, they must learn to integrate their sexuality in a healthy way along with all the other skills they have learned.[20]

It is quite a bit to accomplish; it is no wonder that sometimes we, and they, feel weary and discouraged and overwhelmed. Other times, if we let ourselves, we can share in the exhilaration to be experienced in those shaky first steps out and away. How wonderful to see them embracing the world and moving out into it to make *their* mark and live *their* lives.

It is our job—has been our job—as parents to embrace every stage of our child's growth. Don't stop now! Enjoy them, for this too passes.

Chapter Checkpoints
✔   Allow and encourage safe avenues of separation, also known as rebellion. Teens first discover how to be not like us; then they can discover who they choose to be.
✔   Let go of all that they handle responsibly. Life gets easier and easier—for us.
✔   Include a "No Questions Asked" rescue policy during the teen years.
✔   Strive to work *with* them. It changes their attitude towards you remarkably.
✔   Develop intuition. Listen to yourself.
✔   Teens *are* cool!

Final Thoughts:
Happy Days

Teen Comments

"Teens are more alive than grownups. They have more fun. A lot more fun." —*Tim, 18*

"I get it! All you have to do is be nice to people. They'll be nice back. The one's who aren't nice, aren't happy with themselves. It's amazing how a setback can lead to understanding." —*Katie, 19*

> "Above all, though, children are linked to adults by the simple fact that they are in process of turning into them. For this they may be forgiven much." —Philip Larkin, *Required Writing,* The Savage Seventh

> Having a thirteen-year-old in the family is like having a general admission ticket to the world, to all that is new, to all that is cool.[21]

Being a parent is far more challenging, frustrating, and at times discouraging than anything I have ever done or expected to do. It is also the single most fulfilling and worthwhile thing I have ever done. How can we not at times feel ambivalent toward the job?

It seems that just when I was beginning to get the hang of rearing young children, these same children turned into teens, and the whole ball game changed. I was in left field; I don't know where they were.

Fortunately, I had worked with teens before I had any of my own or else I might have perceived their changes to mean that my sons were not normal. They were all too normal. That which is normal in a teen does not always seem normal to an adult. Luckily as well, I had friends who had children who had already passed through the teen years; these "veteran" mothers were an invaluable source of help, information, practical tips and insight.

I have used the term hormonally challenged quite loosely and most certainly kindly. It came to me the day my thirteen-year-old son asked me three times in less than an hour what day it was. The third time I could not stop myself from saying, "It is still Thursday, Kris." That was the day he generously made a card for one of our friend's five-year-old son and put eleven candles on the cake he had drawn. All of us suffer moments and days where "brain dead" and "brain glitch" rule. In our family, we fondly suggest this is just a "hormonal challenge." I do not wish to offend nor insult anyone with these terms. For us, they are a humorous way to get through the rough days. I include myself in this category, for I find my body, at times, much at the mercy of my own hormones. I have a great deal of empathy for teens. Not only do I remember what it was like to be one, I presently live with unbalanced, fluctuating hormones. This can be an unkind and volatile combination. One group with so many hormones, one with so few.

There is much joy, excitement and laughter shared by teens with us old people. I would go so far as to suggest that one should always maintain contact with at least one teen throughout one's life. Their eyes, not unlike those of a young child, see the world from a unique perspective, a fresh one with so many possibilities and so little cynicism. They are possibility personified. Teens are in the process of falling in love with life. Teens experience life more fully, more intensely than they likely ever will again, certainly more fully than most adults do. Don't be afraid. Spend some time with them. You will learn much and possibly stay a little younger a little longer.

> She discovered with great delight that one does not love one's children just because they are one's children but because of the friendship formed while raising them.
> —Gabriel Garcia Márquez, *Love in the Time of Cholera*

Nothing you do for children is ever wasted. They seem not to notice us, hovering, averting our eyes, and they seldom offer thanks, but what we do for them is never wasted. —Garrison Keillor, *Leaving Home*

About the Author

Madelyn Swift is founder and President of Childright, an educational consulting firm. She is the author of *Discipline for Life: Getting it Right with Children* and numerous articles on dealing with children. She lectures and teaches throughout North America and New Zealand. She is married and has two sons.

For additional information concerning Ms. Swift, please call 1-800-422-4337, or contact us through e-mail at Childright@childright.com, or you may check our website at Childright.com.

1. Marshall, Peter. *Now I Know Why Tigers Eat Their Young: How to Survive Your Teenagers with Humour.* Toronto: Whitecap Books, 1992.

2. I am indebted to Jean Clarke for this observation.

3. *Webster's Seventh New Collegiate Dictionary.* Springfield, MA: G. & C. Merriam Company, 1967

4. I am indebted to Barbara Coloroso for this technique.

5. *Webster's Seventh New Collegiate Dictionary.* Springfield, MA: G. & C. Merriam Company, 1967

6. Swift, M. *Discipline for Life: Getting it Right with Children.* Southlake, TX: Childright, 1999.

7. Anderson, M. *Raising a Family is a Pleasure.* n.d., n.p., out of print. I am indebted to Mike Anderson for sharing this text with me.

8. Swift, M. *Discipline for Life: One Step at a Time* audio tape series. Fort Worth, TX: Stairway Education Programs, 1994.

9. Please see Chapter 10 of Swift, M. *Discipline for Life: Getting it Right with Children.* Southlake, TX: Childright, 1999 for detailed help with problem-solving skills. Problem solving is also addressed in Chapter 10 of this text.

10. I am indebted to Julie O'Keefe for this component of job descriptions of siblings.

11. Pipher, M. *The Shelter of Each Other: Rebuilding Our Families.* NY: G.P. Putnam's Sons, 1996.

12. Swift, M. *Discipline for Life: Getting it Right with Children.* Southlake, TX: Childright, 1999.

13. See text by Dreikurs and Grey, *A New Approach to Discipline: Logical Consequences.* New York: Hawthorn Books, Inc., 1968. I am indebted to these authors for their concept of logical consequences upon which Disciplinary Consequences are based.

14. Swift, M. *Discipline for Life: Getting it Right with Children.* Southlake, TX: Childright, 1999. Please see this text for determination of what does and does not constitute true discipline.

15. Swift, M. *Discipline for Life: Getting it Right with Children.* Southlake, TX: Childright, 1999. This section is based on excerpts from this text.

16. Fisher, R. and Ury, W. *Getting to Yes: Negotiating Agreement Without Giving In.* NY: Penguin Books, 1991.

17. Clarke, J. *Time-In: When Time-Out Doesn't Work.* Parenting Press: Seattle, WA, 1999.

18. Swift, M. *Discipline for Life: Getting it Right with Children.* Southlake, TX: Childright, 1999. This section is based on excerpts from this text.

19. I am indebted to Lynn Deal for this term and insight.

20. Clarke, J. and Connie Dawson. *Growing Up Again: Parenting Ourselves, Parenting Our Children.* New York: Harper/Hazelden, 1989. Please see this wonderful reference for ages and stages and developmental tasks important in each.

21. I am indebted to Max Lerner's "Having a thirteen-year-old in the family is like having a general-admission ticket to the movies, radio and TV." In "Teen-ager," in *New York Post* (4 June 1952).